PROCLAIMING THE TRUMAN DOCTRINE

Library of Presidential Rhetoric

Proclaiming the Truman Doctrine

The Cold War Call to Arms

DENISE M. BOSTDORFF

Texas A&M University Press : College Station

This paper meets the requirements
of ANSI/NISO Z39.48-1992
(Permanence of Paper)
Binding materials have been chosen for durability.

Frontispiece: Harry S. Truman delivers the "Truman Doctrine" speech to Congress, March 12, 1947. Photograph appears courtesy of the Harry S. Truman Presidential Library.

Library of Congress Cataloging-in-Publication Data

Bostdorff, Denise M., 1959–
Proclaiming the Truman Doctrine : the Cold War call to arms / Denise M.
Bostdorff. — 1st ed.
p. cm.—(Library of presidential rhetoric)
Includes bibliographical references and index.
ISBN-13: 978-1-60344-032-5 (cloth : alk. paper)
ISBN-10: 1-60344-032-1 (cloth : alk. paper)
ISBN-13: 978-1-60344-034-9 (pbk. : alk. paper)
ISBN-10: 1-60344-034-8 (pbk. : alk. paper)
1. Truman, Harry S., 1884–1972—Political and social views.   2. Truman,
Harry S., 1884–1972—Oratory.   3. Truman, Harry S., 1884–1972.
Recommendation for assistance to Greece and Turkey.   4. Speeches,
addresses, etc., American—History and criticism.   5. United
States—Foreign relations—1945–1953.   6. Cold War.   7. United
States—Military policy.   8. Truman, Harry S., 1884-1972—Influence.
9. Bush, George W. (George Walker), 1946—Political and social views.
10. United States—Foreign relations—2001–   I. Title.
E814.B67   2008
973.918092—dc22
2007039145

To My Father,

a plain-speaking farmer-politician in his own right

and

To My Mother,

a woman of warmth and gentle forbearance

Contents

Preface

This is a book about politics. It is also a book about words: how humans use words strategically to attain political goals and how, often without us realizing it, words may use us.

Because countless scholars have discussed the Truman Doctrine and a handful have even focused on Truman's speech itself from a rhetorical perspective, one natural question is to ask why we need yet another analysis. My answer is three-fold. First, this study benefits from the passage of time. As the only book-length examination of the Truman Doctrine address, this volume deals far more in-depth with the different forces and individuals that shaped the speech, resolving the questions over authorship that have continued to linger, as well as attending to the multiple levels on which the delivered message served to persuade, including in ways that its authors did not intend. The book draws extensively on archival research, including documents such as George Elsey's addition to his papers at the Truman Library in 2001 and the recently discovered Truman diary released to the public in 2003 that were not available to earlier authors.

Second, this book examines how the Truman Doctrine speech coincided with the rise of public affairs in the State Department, marking the start of officers from policy operations and public information working together in conjunction with the White House to formulate both a foreign policy and the rhetorical strategy needed to sell it publicly. Unlike *Fifteen Weeks,* which gave the celebratory account of a principal—Joseph Jones—involved in the campaign, this volume takes a more dispassionate perspective and, additionally, examines the contributions of both the State Department and the White House.

Finally, this book attempts to shed new light not only on the Truman Doctrine but also on how this event influenced the rhetoric of future U.S. presidents and the historical and political contexts in which they acted. The Truman Doctrine speech, I argue, can best be understood as part of a crisis campaign that established a precedent leading to recurring episodes of presidential foreign crisis promotion and management in the decades that followed. Cold War and post–Cold War presidents would borrow from Truman's rhetoric and from the news management strategies that the U.S. State Department employed in gaining congressional passage of aid to Greece and Turkey. However unintended, the Truman Doctrine speech taught lessons that future administrations would embrace, and its consequences can be seen even in the war on terror.

In the chapters that follow, any italicized words in quoted material—unless otherwise noted—were emphasized in the original. Chapter 4 uses italicized terms in excerpts of the speech as Truman delivered it to indicate words that the president stressed vocally, as revealed by an audio version of the speech available at www.americanrhetoric.com. Other unattributed comments about Truman's delivery that day and the reaction of the audience derive from the viewing of an incomplete newsreel of the speech from the film, *Decision: The Conflicts of Harry S. Truman—Butter and Guns,* available in the Harry S. Truman Library's Motion Picture Collection.

Examining an event after the fact has its perils, of course. As George Elsey, who helped write the Truman Doctrine speech, once grumbled about academics, policymakers "don't sit down and take time to think through and debate ad nauseam all these points. You don't have the time. You've got a job. You've got fifteen or twenty minutes to present your case to the Congress or over the radio to the public, as it was primarily then, . . . and you don't sit around thinking of all the things you can't or shouldn't do." By contrast, scholars can take their time to investigate, so it is easier for them to be critical.

The situation is no different in my case. In this book, I explore, analyze, and critique, knowing that I have the advantage of time and historic perspective to aid me. George Elsey's point is a relevant one, however, as scholars would do well to recognize and appreciate the constraints under which political actors operate. Nonetheless, it is my hope that the political world may also learn from scholars who have the opportunity to reflect more deeply on the significance of political-rhetorical acts and, perhaps, to provide insights that may be drawn upon in the future for practical policymaking.

In completing this scholarly treatment of the Truman Doctrine speech, I owe a special debt to a wide range of individuals who assisted me in ways both large and small. I especially want to thank Martin J. Medhurst, former general editor for the Library of Presidential Rhetoric, for offering me the opportunity to write this volume. From the outset, he appreciated my need to complete this book on a schedule that would allow me to balance my passion for scholarship with my other professional passion of teaching undergraduates at a small liberal arts college. For that I shall be perpetually grateful.

I also wish to thank Ji-Hyun Ahn, Kelly Pang, Kathryn Beck, and Kathryn Gabriele—students who served as my research assistants—as well as the Office of the Vice President for Academic Affairs at the College of Wooster that made their participation in this project possible. Shila Garg, the Dean of the Faculty at Wooster, provided me with two much appreciated Faculty Development Grants for the travel involved in my research.

At the Truman Presidential Library, David Clark, Dennis Bilger, Pauline Testerman, and Liz Safly provided invaluable help. I especially thank Liz, who dealt graciously and effectively with the demands of a large number of researchers and the opening of the 1947 Truman diary during my stay in Independence.

In writing this volume, I also benefited immensely from speaking and corresponding with George M. Elsey, who served as Clark Clifford's assistant at the time of the Truman Doctrine and made significant contributions to the president's speech; Mr. Elsey shared his time and insights generously with me. I would likewise be remiss if I did not acknowledge historian Robert H. Ferrell, who encouraged me in the completion of this project; Kenneth Shafer, MD, a cardiologist at the Cleveland Clinic who cheerfully assisted me in my detective work on Truman's health; and Jake Bostdorff, who made Max and Mabel's place available to me for a few weeks each summer so I would have a peaceful place to think and to write.

I also want to thank my parents, to whom this volume is dedicated. On a daily basis, my mother exemplifies the virtues of listening carefully, acting thoughtfully, and laughing joyfully. Moreover, her example has repeatedly reminded me of how important it is to be kind. To my father, I owe lessons on the values of precision, perseverance, and satisfaction in a job well done. In his own way, he has taught me to examine language critically and to question conventional social wisdom.

Finally, I want to thank my charming Irishman and life's companion, Dan O'Rourke, and our ethnically schizophrenic children: Morgan, who loves history, and Devin, who loves writing. You provided humor, time, and encouragement whenever they were needed and gave far larger gifts that can never be repaid.

Special Message to the Congress on Greece and Turkey: Wednesday, March 12, 1947, 1:00 P.M.

———————————

Mr. President, Mr. Speaker, Members of the Congress of the United States:

The gravity of the situation which confronts the world today necessitates my appearance before a joint session of the Congress.

The foreign policy and the national security of this country are involved.

One aspect of the present situation, which I present to you at this time for your consideration and decision, concerns Greece and Turkey.

The United States has received from the Greek Government an urgent appeal for financial and economic assistance. Preliminary reports from the American Economic Mission now in Greece and reports from the American Ambassador in Greece corroborate the statement of the Greek Government that assistance is imperative if Greece is to survive as a free nation.

I do not believe that the American people and the Congress wish to turn a deaf ear to the appeal of the Greek Government.

Greece is not a rich country. Lack of sufficient natural resources has always forced the Greek people to work hard to make both ends meet. Since 1940, this industrious, peace loving country has suffered invasion, four years of cruel enemy occupation, and bitter internal strife.

When forces of liberation entered Greece they found that the retreating Germans had destroyed virtually all the railways, roads, port facilities, communications, and merchant marine. More than a thousand villages had been burned. Eighty-five percent of the children were tubercular. Livestock, poultry, and draft animals had almost disappeared. Inflation had wiped out practically all savings.

As a result of these tragic conditions, a militant minority, exploiting human want and misery, was able to create political chaos which, until now, has made economic recovery impossible.

Greece is today without funds to finance the importation of those goods which are essential to bare subsistence. Under these circumstances the people of Greece cannot make progress in solving their problems of reconstruction. Greece is in desperate need of financial and economic assistance to enable it to resume purchases of food, clothing, fuel and seeds. These are indispensable for the subsistence of its people and are obtainable only from abroad. Greece must have help to import the goods necessary to restore internal order and security so essential for economic and political recovery.

The Greek Government has also asked for the assistance of experienced American administrators, economists, and technicians to insure that the financial and other aid given to Greece shall be used effectively in creating a stable and self-sustaining economy and in improving its public administration.

The very existence of the Greek state is today threatened by the terrorist activities of several thousand armed men, led by Communists, who defy the government's authority at a number of points, particularly along the northern boundaries. A Commission appointed by the United Nations Security Council is at present investigating disturbed conditions in northern Greece and alleged border violations along the frontier between Greece on the one hand and Albania, Bulgaria, and Yugoslavia on the other.

Meanwhile, the Greek Government is unable to cope with the situation. The Greek army is small and poorly equipped. It needs supplies and equipment if it is to restore authority to the government throughout Greek territory.

Greece must have assistance if it is to become a self-supporting and self-respecting democracy.

The United States must supply this assistance. We have already extended to Greece certain types of relief and economic aid but these are inadequate.

There is no other country to which democratic Greece can turn. No other nation is willing and able to provide the necessary support for a democratic Greek government.

The British Government, which has been helping Greece, can give no further financial or economic aid after March 31. Great Britain finds itself under the necessity of reducing or liquidating its commitments in several parts of the world, including Greece.

We have considered how the United Nations might assist in this crisis. But the situation is an urgent one requiring immediate action, and the United Nations and its related organizations are not in a position to extend help of the kind that is required.

It is important to note that the Greek Government has asked for our aid in utilizing effectively the financial and other assistance we may give to Greece, and in improving its public administration. It is of the utmost importance that we supervise the use of any funds made available to Greece, in such a manner that each dollar spent will count toward making Greece self-supporting, and will help to build an economy in which a healthy democracy can flourish.

No government is perfect. One of the chief virtues of a democracy, however, is that its defects are always visible and under democratic processes can be pointed out and corrected. The government of Greece is not perfect. Nevertheless it represents 85 percent of the members of the Greek Parliament who were chosen in an election last year. Foreign observers, including 692 Americans, considered this election to be a fair expression of the views of the Greek people.

The Greek Government has been operating in an atmosphere of chaos and extremism. It has made mistakes. The extension of aid by this country does not mean that the United States condones everything that the Greek Government has done or will do. We have condemned in the past, and we condemn now, extremist measures of the right or the left. We have in the past advised tolerance, and we advise tolerance now.

Greece's neighbor, Turkey, also deserves our attention.

The future of Turkey as an independent and economically sound state is clearly no less important to the freedom-loving peoples of the world than the future of Greece. The circumstances in which Turkey finds itself today are considerably different from those of Greece. Turkey has been spared the disasters that have beset Greece. And during the war, the United States and Great Britain furnished Turkey with material aid.

Nevertheless, Turkey now needs our support.

Since the war Turkey has sought additional financial assistance from Great Britain and the United States for the purpose of effecting that modernization necessary for the maintenance of its national integrity.

That integrity is essential to the preservation of order in the Middle East.

The British Government has informed us that, owing to its own difficulties, it can no longer extend financial or economic aid to Turkey.

As in the case of Greece, if Turkey is to have the assistance it needs, the United States must supply it. We are the only country able to provide that help.

I am fully aware of the broad implications involved if the United States extends assistance to Greece and Turkey, and I shall discuss these implications with you at this time.

One of the primary objectives of the foreign policy of the United States is the creation of conditions in which we and other nations will be able to work out a way of life free from coercion. This was a fundamental issue in the war with Germany and Japan. Our victory was won over countries which sought to impose their will, and their way of life, upon other nations.

To ensure the peaceful development of nations, free from coercion, the United States has taken a leading part in establishing the United Nations. The United Nations is designed to make possible lasting freedom and independence for all its members. We shall not realize our objectives, however, unless we are willing to help free peoples to maintain their free institutions and their national integrity against aggressive movements that seek to impose upon them totalitarian regimes. This is no more than a frank recognition that totalitarian regimes imposed upon free peoples, by direct or indirect aggression, undermine the foundations of international peace and hence the security of the United States.

The peoples of a number of countries of the world have recently had totalitarian regimes forced upon them against their will. The Government of the United States has made frequent protests against coercion and intimidation, in violation of the Yalta agreement, in Poland, Rumania, and Bulgaria. I must also state that in a number of other countries there have been similar developments.

At the present moment in world history nearly every nation must choose between alternative ways of life. The choice is too often not a free one.

One way of life is based upon the will of the majority, and is distinguished by free institutions, representative government, free elections, guarantees of individual liberty, freedom of speech and religion, and freedom from political oppression.

The second way of life is based upon the will of a minority forcibly imposed upon the majority. It relies upon terror and oppression, a controlled press and radio, fixed elections, and the suppression of personal freedoms.

I believe that it must be the policy of the United States to support free peoples who are resisting attempted subjugation by armed minorities or by outside pressures.

I believe that we must assist free peoples to work out their own destinies in their own way.

I believe that our help should be primarily through economic and financial aid which is essential to economic stability and orderly political processes.

The world is not static, and the status quo is not sacred. But we cannot allow changes in the status quo in violation of the Charter of the United Nations by such methods as coercion, or by such subterfuges as political infiltration. In helping free and independent nations to maintain their freedom, the United States will be giving effect to the principles of the Charter of the United Nations.

It is necessary only to glance at a map to realize that the survival and integrity of the Greek nation are of grave importance in a much wider situation. If Greece should fall under the control of an armed minority, the effect upon its neighbor, Turkey, would be immediate and serious. Confusion and disorder might well spread throughout the entire Middle East.

Moreover, the disappearance of Greece as an independent state would have a profound effect upon those countries in Europe whose peoples are struggling against great difficulties to maintain their freedoms and their independence while they repair the damages of war.

It would be an unspeakable tragedy if these countries, which have struggled so long against overwhelming odds, should lose that victory for which they sacrificed so much. Collapse of free institutions and loss of independence would be disastrous not only for them but for the world. Discouragement and possibly failure would quickly be the lot of neighboring peoples striving to maintain their freedom and independence.

Should we fail to aid Greece and Turkey in this fateful hour, the effect will be far reaching to the West as well as to the East.

We must take immediate and resolute action.

I therefore ask the Congress to provide authority for assistance to Greece and Turkey in the amount of $400,000,000 for the period ending June 30, 1948. In requesting these funds, I have taken into consideration the maximum amount of relief assistance which would be furnished to Greece out of the $350,000,000 which I recently requested that the Congress authorize for the prevention of starvation and suffering in countries devastated by the war.

In addition to funds, I ask the Congress to authorize the detail of American civilian and military personnel to Greece and Turkey, at the request of those countries, to assist in the tasks of reconstruction, and for the purpose of supervising the use of such financial and material assistance as may be furnished. I recommend that authority also be provided for the instruction and training of selected Greek and Turkish personnel.

Finally, I ask that the Congress provide authority which will permit the speediest and most effective use, in terms of needed commodities, supplies, and equipment, of such funds as may be authorized.

If further funds, or further authority, should be needed for the purposes indicated in this message, I shall not hesitate to bring the situation before the Congress. On this subject the Executive and Legislative branches of the Government must work together.

This is a serious course upon which we embark.

I would not recommend it except that the alternative is much more serious.

The United States contributed $341,000,000,000 toward winning World War II. This is an investment in world freedom and world peace.

The assistance that I am recommending for Greece and Turkey amounts to little more than 1/10 of 1 percent of this investment. It is only common sense that we should safeguard this investment and make sure that it was not in vain.

The seeds of totalitarian regimes are nurtured by misery and want. They spread and grow in the evil soil of poverty and strife. They reach their full growth when the hope of a people for a better life has died.

We must keep that hope alive.

The free peoples of the world look to us for support in maintaining their freedoms.

If we falter in our leadership, we may endanger the peace of the world—and we shall surely endanger the welfare of this Nation.

Great responsibilities have been placed upon us by the swift movement of events.

I am confident that the Congress will face these responsibilities squarely.[1]

CHAPTER 1

Prelude to Cold War Crisis

Wednesday, March 12, 1947, was a warm and welcoming day, appreciated all the more by residents of Washington, D.C., after two major snowstorms in recent weeks had nearly brought the city to a standstill. One storm had even forced Pres. Harry Truman to abandon his usual early-morning walk.[1]

On March 12, the mild weather promised the arrival of spring, but this optimistic expectation contrasted sharply with anticipation of a very different sort about the president's address to Congress scheduled for that afternoon.

For weeks, newspaper, magazine, and radio coverage had been saturated with chilling stories that foreshadowed a dramatic change in the U.S. relationship with its wartime ally, the Soviet Union, change marked by an impending crisis in the Mediterranean. Newspapers reported on February 28 that Great Britain had informed the United States that it could no longer continue to provide military and economic support to the Greek government, which was in danger of falling to Communist rebels. In turn, Truman had met privately with congressional leaders to request that the United States assume Britain's burden.[2] After the sacrifices of World War II and the tumult of the postwar economy, most Americans had little interest in involvement abroad. Yet media reports in the weeks leading up to the president's speech emphasized the danger of the situation and how urgent it was for the United States to check Soviet expansion. An editorial in *Newsweek*, for example, opined, "If Greece is lost, a Communist scythe will curve around the head of Turkey, which already has Communist bayonets at its back. Russia would, or could, control the Eastern Mediterranean." In his March 7 commentary, ABC's Earl Godwin told listeners that "somebody has got to do something and they're all looking at your Uncle Sam." A *New York Times* headline went so far as to declare, "Survival of Western Civilization Is Held to Depend on Our Actions."[3] Still, there had been no direct word from the president himself on the matter. After nearly two weeks of news coverage devoted to the issue, citizens, journalists, and members of Congress anxiously awaited Truman's speech. As an editorial in the *Washington Daily News* expressed, "We hope President Truman's expected statement on the Greek crisis will take the American people fully and frankly into his confidence."[4]

At 1600 Pennsylvania Avenue, the Truman White House also was highly aware of the import of the moment. Eben Ayers, assistant press secretary to the president, walked to the South Portico where cars had arrived to transport the presidential party to Capitol Hill. The president got into his car at 12:40 P.M., accompanied by his aides and Adm. William Leahy, but when the president saw Ayers, he had the car door opened so that he could shake Ayers's hand. Bess Truman and Margaret Strickler, Margaret Truman's music teacher, no sooner entered the second car than Mrs. Truman discovered that she did not have her card for the congressional gallery. A Midwesterner to her core, the First Lady never wanted others to feel she was taking advantage of her position, so the oversight flustered her. Eventually, however, Mrs. Truman accepted the assurances of a White House usher, Wilson Surles, that her omission was not a problem. The third car of the procession carried Charlie Ross, the president's press secretary and friend since their youth in Independence, Missouri; William Hassett, correspondence secretary; John Steelman, assistant to the president; Matt Connelly, appointments secretary; George Schoeneman, commissioner of internal revenue; and Clark Clifford, special counsel. According to Ayers, Margaret Truman also came to see everyone off, handkerchiefs strategically placed over her head and around her throat for protection since she was recovering from bronchial pneumonia. Margaret empathized with her father's nerves because she suffered from stage fright herself and was awaiting her radio debut as a coloratura soprano. As the cars pulled away, Margaret said to Ayers, "I know how Daddie feels."[5]

The president and his party reached the Capitol a few minutes later to find it crowded not only with members of Congress but also with distinguished guests and, dressed gaily for spring in correspondence with the weather, "all the wives of high officialdom who could wrangle a ticket from their husbands," as the State Department's Joseph Jones would later put it. The uplifting splash of spring color aside, however, the atmosphere was grim as audience members anticipated the critical nature of Truman's speech, the major arguments of which had circulated freely in the media in the preceding days. Bess Truman and Margaret Strickler tried to make their way to their front row seats but without a great deal of success, eventually prompting a White House aide to announce the First Lady's arrival in order to clear a path. A few minutes before 1:00 P.M., the doorkeeper announced members of the cabinet, who entered the chamber. They were followed by Senators Tom Connally, Robert Taft, and Wallace White, and Representatives Charles Halleck, Charles Eaton, and Sam Rayburn, who all escorted the president.[6]

As Truman made his way down the center aisle, dressed sharply in a dark blue suit, he paused at the sight of a blonde, seven-year-old girl who was in the aisle, the daughter of Rep. Thomas Abernathy, an opponent of the New Deal from Mississippi. Her hands were clutching a notepad and pencil intended to keep her occupied during the president's speech. When he came to her, Truman bowed, shook her hand, and said hello. A few moments later, he stopped again to shake hands with Rep. Joseph Mansfield, age 86, who was seated in a wheelchair. Observers recalled that the president appeared glum, drawn, and somber.[7] No doubt the importance of the moment weighed heavily on him. What many observers did not know, however, was that Truman was feeling poorly that day. While he had always been prone to suffer from stress, the president was also still recovering from an upper respiratory infection that had plagued him since late January. The combination of stress and illness had taken its toll, sapping Truman of his usual energy.[8]

When he reached the podium, the president opened the black loose-leaf notebook that he typically used for formal presentations and took a long drink of water. Then Truman looked at his audience, his blue eyes enlarged by his thick eyeglasses, and began to speak. "Mr. President, Mr. Speaker, Members of the Congress of the United States," he intoned in a voice that was slightly hoarse. "The gravity of the situation which confronts the world today necessitates my appearance before a joint session of the Congress. The foreign policy and the national security of this country are involved." In the nineteen minutes that followed, Truman spoke at a rate that was slower than his usual pace and more deliberate, as he detailed for his listeners how the Greek government, besieged by the "terrorist activities of several thousand armed men, led by Communists," was on the verge of falling. The president not only argued that the United States should help Greece and neighboring Turkey but also made a more sweeping statement of policy. According to Truman, "I believe it must be the policy of the United States to support free peoples who are resisting attempted subjugation by armed minorities or by outside pressures." The president claimed that inaction on the part of the United States could lead to the "collapse of free institutions and loss of independence [in Greece and Turkey that] would be disastrous not only for them but for the world."[9] Truman's address articulated a new policy—the Truman Doctrine—and marked a turning point in U.S. foreign policy, setting a new course for the nation's relationship with the Soviet Union and with the world. As a call to Cold War crisis, the speech also would have far-reaching consequences that represented both the best of the United States—the Marshall Plan—and its worst—the arms race and repeated military intervention abroad. This book seeks to understand the rhetoric of Truman's address, as well as the corresponding persuasive campaign of which it was a part.

The Truman Doctrine Speech as a Crisis Campaign

The fact that the Truman Doctrine speech depicted a momentous decision through the language of urgency and disease (the "collapse" of Greece and need to stop the "spread" of Communism) is not surprising once one looks at the etymology of the term *crisis*. According to the *Oxford English Dictionary, crisis* refers to "the turning-point of a disease for better or worse," to "a conjunction of the planets which determines the issue of a disease or critical point in the course of events," and to a "vitally important or decisive stage in the progress of anything."[10] The rhetoric of crisis is seductive, for it strives to frighten its audience, typically depicting the world in black and white terms rather than shades of gray and serves to justify particular policies as the only course of action possible by arguing that time is of the essence if devastating consequences are to be avoided.

In this book, I argue that the Truman Doctrine speech can best be understood as part of a concerted crisis campaign that set the stage for routine episodes of presidential foreign crisis promotion and management in the decades that followed. Cold War and post–Cold War presidents have frequently made use of rhetoric to convince citizens that a crisis existed or to magnify crisis perceptions that already were held. By doing so, they have attempted to create a sense of urgency sufficient to legitimize their foreign policy resolutions.[11] The Truman Doctrine speech and accompanying campaign served as a prelude to these later events.

Generative and Strategic Functions of Rhetoric

By examining the Truman Doctrine speech and the administration's related communication efforts as a crisis campaign, I am *not* arguing that Truman and his administration dealt with rhetoric rather than reality, for these are not opposed concepts. Zarefsky explained their relationship when he said, "Rhetoric is not different from reality; it is a set of choices that invites us to see one reality rather than another."[12] For example, individuals armed with weapons may exist, but the terms we use to describe them—"Communist guerillas" versus "freedom fighters"—help to construct two very different realities, as well as point the way to distinctly different policies as the best way to deal with those realities. In their fine but often overlooked volume, *The Cold War as Rhetoric,* Hinds and Windt argued that the Cold War in the United States was largely a "rhetorically constructed ideological reality that was first accepted within the ruling circles of government, then publicly conveyed through major speeches and writings to Americans who generally accepted it as the reality of both foreign and domestic politics."[13] The rhetorical dimensions of the Cold War become clear, Medhurst held, when one examines past policy decisions made by intelligent government officials who drew on the evidence at hand. "That we today can see flaws in the Munich analogy and the domino theory simply underscores the point: reality did not change, only our ability to read and interpret that reality—a reality *that was our own construction in the first place.*"[14] Hence, the language that policymakers use themselves to talk and write about issues, whether intentional or not, has an impact upon their perceptions of reality. In turn, they often unconsciously convey these depictions of reality to journalists and citizens through their communication with these individuals. Simply choosing to speak about troop movements in a country far from our shores heightens the perceived importance of events there. Likewise, a president may believe that a Caribbean coup is a "crisis" and call it by that name, thereby influencing others to see the event in the same way.

Foreign policy in general and the Cold War in particular are also rhetorical in the sense that Aristotle described: "the faculty of observing in any given case the available means of persuasion." That is, rhetoric can also be strategic or a means to an end.[15] Truman in 1947 had no individuals on his staff devoted solely to speechwriting or the art of strategic rhetoric. Rather, as George Elsey, Clark Clifford's assistant in the Truman White House and one of the chief architects of the Truman Doctrine speech, recalled, he was a "Jack-of-many-trades," one of which included speechwriting.[16] And while Elsey may not have been conscious of how terminological choices in the discussion of policy could subtly influence the perceptions of those in government and those without, he did recognize the strategic uses of rhetoric. Elsey told an interviewer in 1969 that his job as a speechwriter had been taking "the hard facts and problems the President of the United States had to cope with and setting those forth in words that would appeal and could be understood by the American people at large."[17] Analysis of the Truman Doctrine reveals how rhetoric functioned both generatively to shape perceptions of reality and strategically to win public and congressional approval for a new presidential policy.

Conclusion

In late February 1947, the U.S. State Department learned that Great Britain intended to end its aid to Greece and Turkey, a shift in policy that might well lead to the demise of the Greek government. The corruption of the reactionary government, including its violation of civil liberties and refusal to implement economic reforms, did not necessitate that its fall be perceived as a mortal threat to democracy, nor its need for aid as a monumental crisis.[18] Yet this is exactly how Under Secretary of State Dean Acheson, especially, and other members of the administration understood the issue. They then quickly mounted an elaborate effort at strategic rhetoric to persuade others—members of Congress, journalists, and citizens—to their point of view. Through the nature of their congressional consultations and through news management—an effort made possible by the State Department's new focus on "public affairs"—members of the Truman administration made adroit use of advance work for the speech. The address itself emphasized the ideas and characteristics of crisis established in the pre-speech congressional and media conditioning. As a result, the Truman administration's rhetoric served as a benchmark, establishing the themes, lines of argument, and language that would appear in presidential foreign crisis rhetoric for decades to come. Even in the war on terror, the Truman Doctrine's impact persists.

CHAPTER 2

Turning Points, 1945–47

Although it is impossible to provide here a complete analysis of the postwar context in which the president spoke, some understanding of the political and rhetorical turning points that led to Truman's speech on March 12, 1947, is essential. The change in U.S. policy that Truman announced may have seemed sudden to many observers, but the truth was that the president had slowly been making up his mind about the Soviets for more than a year. As several authors have noted, Truman was committed to Wilsonian idealism, which argued the only way international peace could be achieved was if world powers in ideological conflict with one another could find a way to cooperate; simultaneously, the president believed—in Hamby's words—that "power was the ultimate arbiter in relations among nations." The history of the world wars initially supported Truman's Wilsonian point of view, but a number of incidents with the Soviet Union over the time period of 1945–47 eventually convinced him that the principles of democracy and peace could only be realized if a power balance of some kind could be established between the East and the West.[1] As this chapter will show, rhetoric played a major role in shaping Truman's ultimate perspective.

Tensions Emerge: February–October 1945

That the American public was largely unaware of the evolution in Truman's thinking until March 1947 can be attributed to what Medhurst termed Truman's "reticence." That is, until he had his mind made up, the president largely chose to remain silent about troubling developments in U.S.-Soviet relations, thereby making it unclear as to exactly where he stood.[2] And there was no shortage of troubling developments. In 1945, for example, after the Soviets unilaterally moved Poland's boundaries westward by 150 miles, an act that gave the USSR additional territory and shifted a comparable amount of territory from Germany to Poland, Britain and the United States could only accede to the fait accompli. At Yalta, Stalin had agreed to democratic elections in Poland, but when he showed no sign of allowing them Truman sent Roosevelt's old emissary, Harry Hopkins, to meet with Stalin in May 1945 to enforce the pledge. Although a few minor concessions were made and the United States decided to recognize the new Polish government, the Soviets largely had their way. The same basic story was repeated in Rumania and Bulgaria. Moreover, discord developed among the Allies over the degree to which war reparations should be exacted from Germany and how they should be collected. The result of these conflicts was to push the United States and Great Britain closer together and away from the USSR.[3]

By the fall of 1945, evidence of the developing fissures began to appear. President Truman, in his October 27 Navy Day speech, stated several fundamentals of U.S. foreign policy, including: "We believe that all peoples who are prepared for self-government should be permitted to choose their own form of government by their own freely expressed choice, without interference from any foreign source." This principle would later reappear in the Truman Doctrine speech, yet its inclusion in the president's 1945 address did not obviously point a finger at the Soviets since Truman's explicit references to them were positive. In the Navy Day message, the president declared, "The people in the United States, in Russia, and Britain, in France and China, in collaboration with all the other peace-loving people, must take the course of current history into their own hands and mold it in a new direction—the direction of continued cooperation." This passage not only depicted the Soviets as interested in peace like other U.S. allies but also demonstrated well Truman's faith that Wilsonian idealism might yet prevail. Four days after the president's speech, Secretary of State James Byrnes spoke before the New York *Herald-Tribune* forum where he, too, expressed U.S. support for democracy and people's right to self-rule while also noting that the United States "sympathized" with the Soviets' "special security concerns" in Central and Eastern Europe.[4] In sum, while Truman and Byrnes both included jabs at the Soviet Union in their messages, their criticism was implicit, rather than direct, and they also coupled it with words of support for the Soviets. No new line toward the USSR was yet clear.

Stalin's Election-Eve Address: February 9, 1946

On February 9, 1946, Stalin caused even more consternation in Washington officialdom with a speech given the night before a Soviet election, a speech that clearly was not needed for him to win at the polls. Instead, according to Hinds and Windt, "the speech was intended to reassert the fundamental values upon which Soviet society was based, Marxist-Leninism" and hence marked a transition to peacetime. While Stalin had relied on nationalistic appeals during the war in order to unite Soviet citizens against the Nazis, he needed to reinvigorate internal commitment to Communism now that the war was over. The first 10 percent of his speech emphasized how "the anti-fascist coalition of the Soviet Union, the United States of America, Great Britain and other freedom-loving states" had triumphed and also declared that the outcome of the war proved the Soviet system's "unquestionable vitality" as "a form of organization . . . superior to any non-Soviet social order." In the remainder of the speech, Stalin defended the performance of the Soviet army and economy during the war. He then laid out the details of a new Five-Year Plan intended to accelerate achievements in both agriculture and heavy industry.[5]

Some officials in Washington, D.C.—including Under Secretary of State Dean Acheson, recently retired U.S. ambassador to Moscow Averell

Harriman, and Pres. Harry Truman himself—saw nothing particularly sinister in what Stalin had to say. Rather, they viewed his message as an address directed at an internal audience purely for political purposes. As Truman reflected upon Stalin's words during an appearance of his own at the Women's Press Club, "Well, you know we always have to demagogue a little, before elections."[6]

Others, however, felt differently. In his diary, Navy Secretary James Forrestal recorded asking Supreme Court Justice William O. Douglas for his impression of Stalin's speech. Douglas replied that it was the "Declaration of World War III," an assessment that Forrestal circulated widely in an effort to undermine a cooperative U.S. policy toward the USSR.[7]

In his address, Stalin had made a number of assertions that were interpreted as threats. He noted, for instance, that he was certain "if we give our scientists proper assistance they will be able in the near future not only to overtake but to surpass the achievements of science beyond the boundaries of our country." For some officials, this statement clearly seemed directed at breaking the United States' lock on the atomic bomb. The report, two weeks after Stalin's speech, that Canada had arrested nearly two dozen people for spying to gain atomic secrets added credence to such concerns. In addition, Stalin had asserted that the USSR must triple its steel production by 1960 since "Only under such conditions can we consider that our homeland will be guaranteed against all possible accidents." The most widely distributed English version of the speech translated the last word of the latter sentence not as "accidents" but as "eventualities," a phrase that implied events that the USSR might instigate, rather than mishaps over which the Soviets would have no control. The lofty goals and term "eventualities" suggested a conflict with the West to some government officials, particularly within the State Department. However, Adam Ulam pointed out that Stalin's statement, quite to the contrary, indicated weakness because it revealed that the Soviets were not ready in 1946 for a major conflict and that they did not anticipate such "eventualities" until at least 1960. Anxious Western officials also overlooked how far the USSR was behind the United States industrially after the damage of the war.

Although a *New York Times* headline blared that Stalin's goals were "near ours," Frank Costigliola observed that "the *Times*'s own figures cited U.S. production in 1944 of sixty-one million tons of pig iron and ninety million tons of steel, both of which well exceeded Stalin's 1960 projections." The director of European Affairs in the State Department, Herbert Mathews, remained so concerned about the speech, however, that he recommended to Byrnes that George Kennan at the Moscow embassy provide an analysis of Stalin's message and what it might mean for future planning.[8]

Kennan's Long Telegram: February 22, 1946

Clearly, U.S. policy toward the Soviet Union had not yet changed, but movement was occurring—movement that Kennan would accelerate. When the request reached him, Kennan, the *charge d'affaires* at the Moscow embassy after Harriman's resignation, was bedridden with a variety of ailments: fever, sinus, toothache, and the side effects of sulfa drugs that he had been prescribed. Nevertheless, Kennan saw the request as an opportunity to have his voice heard after a frustrating eighteen months in which he had tried to convince U.S. officials of the merits of his views on the Soviets. In his memoirs, Kennan would recall, "They had asked for it. Now, by God, they would have it." He called for his secretary and then, from his sickbed, dictated a telegram of over eight thousand words. As Kennan later described it, the message was "neatly divided, like an eighteenth-century Protestant sermon, into five separate parts" in the hope that the divisions would make the telegram appear shorter than it was.[9]

Transmitted on February 22, 1946, the Long Telegram explained Soviet behavior in terms of Russian nationalism and security fears, much like other recent reports within the State Department by Charles Bohlen, Cloyce Huston, and Bohlen and Geroid Robinson.[10] However, it also emphasized to a degree that no one had until then the role of ideology. According to Kennan, "international Marxism, with its honeyed promises to a desperate and war-torn outside world" made Russian nationalism "more dangerous and insidious than ever before."

He explained that Communism would lead the Soviets, on the official level, to strengthen their position as much as possible by developing their military and industry, enlarging their armed forces, expanding their influence by establishing friendly governments, undermining Western influence on colonies and "backward or dependent peoples," and developing positive ties with nations likely to oppose the West. More frightening, however, were Kennan's assertions about Soviet policies that could be expected on "an unofficial or subterranean plane." His message warned that Moscow had already infiltrated the inner core of Communist parties in other countries in a "tightly coordinated and directed" campaign to spread Communism. In addition, Kennan provided a long list of groups subject to possible "penetration" by Communists: labor unions, youth groups, cultural groups, women's and civil rights organizations, liberal publications, the Eastern Orthodox Church, and governments such as those in Yugoslavia and Bulgaria. He argued that the Soviets also would attempt to "disrupt national self-confidence" and "stimulate all forms of disunity" in the West by pitting groups against one another on issues such as class and race and by pitting the Western powers against each other. If Soviet purposes were thwarted by a particular government, Soviet underground forces would even go so far as to work toward the removal of that government. "In summary," Kennan wrote, "we have here a political force committed fanatically to the belief that with us there can be no permanent *modus vivendi*, that it is desirable and necessary that the internal harmony of our society be disrupted, our traditional way of life be destroyed, the international authority of our state be broken, if Soviet power is to be secure."[11]

After presenting this horrific vision of the future, Kennan tried to reassure the recipients of his message that U.S. problems with the Soviets could be solved "without recourse to any general military conflict." He observed that the Soviet government, unlike Nazi Germany, was predisposed against unnecessary risk and would likely back down whenever it met with resistance. In addition, Kennan stated that the Western world had more "cohesion, firmness, and vigor" than the USSR, that the long-term survival of the Soviet system was not yet a given, and that the negative nature of Soviet propaganda could easily be fought "by any intelligent and really constructive program." Kennan closed his Long Telegram by urging greater study of the Soviets, better education of the public, resolution of problems within our own society, more positive projection of a democratic world to motivate other nations, and care that, in dealing with Soviet Communism, the United States not become like the enemy that it faced.[12]

At a number of points within his message, Kennan attempted to calm his audience's fears and warned against excessive emotionalism. He wrote, for instance, "I am convinced that there would be far less hysterical anti-Sovietism in our country today if realities of this situation were better understood." The language and style of Kennan's telegram, however, worked against the very rationality that he urged. From his own sickbed, he had regularly engaged in metaphors of disease and health to describe the U.S.-Soviet relationship. For instance, he asserted, "Much depends on [the] health and vigor of our own society. World communism is like [a] malignant parasite which feeds only on diseased tissues." Indeed, Ivie argued that Kennan had a habit of emotionally projecting his own physical illnesses "onto the external world of politics," thereby depicting a world far more imperiled than it really was. More than twenty years after the Long Telegram, Kennan himself seemed to recognize that his choices in terminology and style had undermined his call for a reasoned approach to dealing with Soviet behavior. Kennan recounted that he had read the Long Telegram in preparing his memoirs "with a horrified amusement. Much of it reads exactly like one of those primers put out by alarmed congressional committees or by the Daughters of the American Revolution, designed to arouse the citizenry to the dangers of the Communist conspiracy."[13]

Kennan's Long Telegram would have exactly that kind of impact, not on the citizenry as a whole, but on government officials behind the scenes who read it. After examining the missive, Secretary of State Byrnes thanked Kennan for his "splendid analysis." Mathews deemed it "Magnificent!" and State's Loy Henderson, who would later play a significant role in crafting the administration's response to Greece, declared that Kennan "hits the nail on the head." While Acheson found Kennan's policy recommendations less than helpful, the under secretary of state judged that "his predictions and warnings could not have been better." Based on these positive responses, the State Department distributed the Long Telegram to its offices and diplomatic missions. Kennan's analysis resonated especially well with Forrestal, who obtained a copy from Harriman and, in turn, gave copies of it to hundreds of colleagues, acquaintances, and military officers.[14] Kennan subsequently observed that his missive had its effect primarily due to its timing; had the telegram arrived earlier, it would have met with disapproval, but had it arrived much later, Kennan's analysis would have been akin to preaching to the choir. "All this only goes to show that more important than the observable nature of external reality, when it comes to the determination of Washington's view of the world, is the subjective state of readiness on the part of Washington officialdom to recognize this or that feature of it." The episode also energized Kennan's career. After the Long Telegram, he concluded, "My reputation was made. My voice now carried."[15]

The Long Telegram did not lead immediately to a change in U.S. foreign policy, but it planted the seeds for such a change. For a long time, historians could find no evidence that Truman had read Kennan's missive, and even members of the administration provided no definitive proof. Elsey, however, had been troubled by Truman's lack of alarm over Soviet behavior and recalled passing Kennan's missive to the president. In October 2003, he looked through his files at the Truman Library in search of evidence to support his memory. There Elsey found his copy of the Long Telegram, bearing the initials of Admiral Leahy and a "P" to indicate that after Elsey and Leahy had talked about it, that Leahy had discussed Kennan's report with the president.[16] While Truman was familiar with Kennan's analysis, however, his reaction to it is unknown. Nonetheless, the Long Telegram appeared both to reflect and spur evolutions in thought that were already underway.

On February 27, just five days after the transmittal of the Long Telegram, Republican senator Arthur Vandenberg of Michigan delivered a blistering speech on the floor of the Senate. A convert to internationalism after Pearl Harbor and a delegate to the U.N. Charter conference, Vandenberg urged the administration to be tougher with the Soviets. He asserted that "we can live together in reasonable harmony if the United States speaks as plainly upon all occasions as Russia does; if the United States just as vigorously sustains its own purposes and its ideals upon all occasions as Russia does." Moreover, Vandenberg warned, "There is a line beyond which compromise cannot go."[17]

Byrnes responded the next day with what some journalists impiously called "the Second Vandenberg Concerto," a speech before the Overseas Press Club in New York. According to Byrnes, Truman had enthusiastically approved the text in advance. In clear allusions to U.S.-Soviet relations, the secretary of state said, "All around us there is suspicion and distrust, which in turn breeds suspicion and distrust. Some suspicions are unfounded and unreasonable. Of some others that cannot be said." Nonetheless, Byrnes noted that the United States had welcomed the Soviet Union into the family of nations. "Despite the differences in our way of life, our people admire and respect our Allies and wish to continue to be friends and partners in a world of expanding freedom and rising standards of living." Byrnes cautioned, though, that the U.N. Charter required that its signatories forsake aggression and emphasized that "in the interest of world peace and in the interest of our common and traditional friendship we must make it plain that the United States intends to defend the Charter." Byrnes was aggravated with the Soviets since his recent meetings in Moscow had resulted in no substantial movement on the part of the USSR in regard to Rumania and Bulgaria and, despite the uneasy relationship that he and Truman often had, his boss undoubtedly shared his frustration, as did others like Vandenberg. Nonetheless, it seems likely that Kennan's Long Telegram also played a role in encouraging Byrnes's public toughness by giving voice to the fears that many American officials—including those in State, in the White House, and even in Congress—were beginning to harbor.[18]

Churchill's Westminster Address: March 5, 1946

The transmission of Kennan's message was quickly followed, on March 5, by Winston Churchill's address at Westminster College in Fulton, Missouri, in which he took a similar tack. In the fall of 1945, the president of Westminster College, Frank McCluer, had invited Churchill to speak there on his upcoming vacation to the United States. Gen. Harry Vaughn, Truman's military aide, had been a Westminster classmate of McCluer and showed the invitation to the president who then decided to add a line of his own. Truman wrote, "Dear Winnie. This is a fine old college out in my state. If you'll come out and make them a speech, I'll take you out and introduce you." Churchill immediately accepted.[19]

In his address, the former prime minister declared, "From Stettin in the Baltic to Trieste in the Adriatic, an iron curtain has descended across the Continent. Behind that line lie all the capitals of the ancient states of Central and Eastern Europe." Churchill's use of the metaphor, "iron curtain," at Fulton drew widespread public attention simply because Truman had introduced him, but the phrase had actually been around much longer. In the 1920s, it referred to how the Communist Revolution had ended the Westernization of Russia and, in the waning days of World War II, Joseph Goebbels relied on "iron curtain" to encourage the Germans to fight, rather than face Soviet occupation. Churchill, too, had begun using the phrase in 1945 in reference to the USSR. By November of that year, Vandenberg had picked up the term and included "iron curtain" in a speech in the U.S. Senate. Churchill's Westminster address not only invoked the metaphor again, but—presaging the future—underscored the importance of Greece. Behind the iron curtain, he intoned, "Athens alone—Greece with its immortal glories—is free to decide its future at an election under British, American and French observation."[20]

Like Kennan, the British statesman also cautioned his American audience about "fifth columns [that] constitute a growing challenge and peril to Christian civilisation." Churchill added further urgency to his depiction by making an analogy between the current postwar circumstances and those of Munich. As he recalled, "Last time I saw it all coming and cried aloud to my own fellow-countrymen and to the world, but no one paid any attention. . . . and one by one we were all sucked into the awful whirlpool. We surely must not let that happen again." Although Churchill expressed hope that the fledgling United Nations might promote understanding with the Russians, he made clear that an alliance between English-speaking peoples of the British Commonwealth and the United States was essential for peace. He ended his address by underscoring the need for such a coalition and by alluding to Neville Chamberlain's infamous "peace in our time" concession to Hitler: "[I]f all British moral and material forces and convictions are joined with your own in fraternal association, the high-roads of the future will be clear, not only for us but for all, not only for our time, but for a century to come."[21]

Churchill's speech met with mixed reactions. In Great Britain, the press both praised and condemned it, but the diplomatic community was highly—although privately in Foreign Secretary Ernest Bevin's case—enthusiastic. In the United States, Congress and the press also responded in widely divergent ways, but public opinion appeared overwhelmingly against Churchill's proposition and against the president's apparent approval of it.[22] Now that the war was over, anti-British sentiment had resumed, and Americans were in no mood to hear another call to arms, particularly from a nation that many U.S. citizens perceived as a colonial bully.

In a matter of days, Churchill's speech had become a major embarrassment to Truman, and he quickly distanced himself and the administration from it. Reporters questioned the president about the matter at a March 8 news conference, but Truman insisted that he had not known what would be in Churchill's address, a statement that simply was not true. As early as February 10, Churchill had been in conversation with the president and Admiral Leahy about the topic of his speech. Byrnes had read the address and given Truman a summary, which did not alarm the president, and Truman received a copy on the train to Fulton. In further response to reporters' questions, the president said, "This is a country of free speech. Mr. Churchill had a perfect right to say what he pleased." When a reporter pressed the issue further, asking Truman for his opinion of Churchill's message, he responded, "I have no comment." Acheson, who was to represent the administration at Churchill's farewell reception in New York, cancelled with the explanation that urgent matters necessitated he stay in Washington, D.C. Years later, Byrnes would write that the president had strategically chosen not to read the text himself so that he could, if necessary, disavow advance knowledge of its contents. Elsey maintained that "Truman's own ambivalence" led the president to distance himself from Churchill's speech.[23]

In an interview with *Pravda* on March 13, Stalin criticized Churchill's address, charging that its proposition of an Anglo-American alliance was similar to Hitler's racial appeals, yet, significantly, Stalin did not attack the United States. Truman, in his turn, sent word to Stalin that he would gladly give the Soviet leader the chance to speak at the University of Missouri at Columbia if Stalin were so inclined.[24] Although the president may have agreed with much that Churchill said, he still was not ready to break with the Soviets completely, both because his commitment to Wilsonian idealism continued to beckon him and because he perceived that domestic opinion was not yet ready for such a shift. Truman therefore backed away from Churchill's Fulton speech, but events soon showed that administration policy toward the Soviet Union had continued to evolve in a direction more hospitable to Churchill's point of view than to Stalin's.

Events in Iran and Turkey: March–September 1946

Indeed, to understand fully the messages from Kennan, Vandenberg, Byrnes, and Churchill in late February and early March 1946, one also has to appreciate another event that was unfolding at the same time in Iran. British and Soviet troops had first occupied Iran in August 1941 in order to secure a supply route to the Soviet Union, with American troops arriving the following year to help. Although the 1942 treaty of alliance, to which the United States was not a party, aimed to limit intrusion into Iran's internal affairs and to protect its sovereignty after the war, the Iranians had, from the start, taken every step they could to lay the groundwork for American intervention. Stephen McFarland described the situation well: "Iranians hated the British and feared the Soviets, making it more necessary to employ a third-power ... to create a buffer between Iran and the occupiers." To carry out this strategy, the Iranians asked for American advisers to reform its military and police and to run its railway and government industries, tried to attract American oil interests to the country, and—even from the perspective of the American minister—consistently sent exaggerated accounts of Soviet misbehavior to the American government.[25]

Tensions began building in the fall of 1944 when the Soviet Union officially joined Great Britain and the United States in the competition for an oil concession in northern Iran. Having painted itself into a corner, the Iranian government could not afford to award the concession to the Americans over the Soviets and quickly announced that it was postponing all negotiations until the war had ended. The Soviets took umbrage with this decision since its timing appeared to be anti-Soviet and U.S. petroleum geologists were serving as oil advisors to the Iranian government. Moreover, the Soviets and the Iranians had signed a treaty in 1921 that terminated a Russian oil concession in northern Iran, with the condition that the concession never be given to any other government. The USSR had also told the Iranians in 1941 that it objected to American companies holding concessions in Iran entirely. When the Iranian government closed down negotiations in 1944, the Soviets retaliated by using the Tudeh Communist party to launch public protests against the government, stopping traffic going into and out of Soviet-occupied Azerbaijan, and making overt threats. The Soviets stopped only when the government officials responsible for the postponement in the concession negotiations resigned and when the United States expressed support for the Iranian government through a note that Kennan delivered to Soviet foreign minister Vyacheslav Molotov.[26]

In 1945, as it had historically, the Iranian government refused to improve its treatment of northern minorities and, instead, employed the military to suppress them, along with leftists all over Iran. The

USSR encouraged rebellion, which contributed to the December 1945 formation of the Autonomous Republic of Azerbaijan and the Kurdish People's Republic. In response, the Iranian government charged that the Soviets were the sole cause of its domestic unrest. Hossein 'Ala, the new Iranian ambassador to the United States, pressed for Iran's case to be heard by the U.N. Security Council, calling the Soviets "contagious bacilli." As a show of support for Iran and nearby Turkey who was also feeling threatened, Truman sent the battleship *Missouri* to Istanbul to return the remains of the Turkish ambassador to the United States with honor, and, as Ayers surmised in his diary, to impress the Soviets with U.S. military might. Although the Soviet Union had agreed with the Allies to withdraw its troops from Iran by March 2, 1946, it did not do so, and reports circulated that the Soviets were moving more troops into Iran. Truman, clearly exasperated, directed the new U.S. ambassador to Moscow, Walter Bedell Smith, "to tell Stalin I had always held him to be a man to keep his word. Troops in Iran after Mar. 2 upset that theory." Publicly, the president was restrained. When a reporter asked what his plans were if the Russians did not withdraw, Truman said simply, "That is a matter that will be handled when it comes up."[27]

Although the context of the Iranian crisis was more complex than most American officials recognized, events in Iran, nonetheless, make it easier to understand how those officials interpreted Stalin's February 9 speech as a bellicose threat and to appreciate further the events spurring the warnings of Kennan, Vandenberg, Byrnes, and Churchill. The secretary of state, after meeting privately with Churchill for over two hours on March 11, would reinforce his February 28 comments to the Overseas Press Club in an address delivered on March 16 in New York City before the Society of the Friendly Sons of Saint Patrick. Byrnes avoided any mention of Soviet responsibility for the Iranian crisis, but he again made a clear statement of U.S. intentions by focusing on the purpose of U.S. military strength. According to the secretary of state, "The United States is committed to the support of the charter of the United Nations. Should the occasion arise, our military strength will be used to support the purpose and the principles of the charter." Byrnes also presented the U.S. argument on behalf of Iran at the U.N.

Security Council on March 26, whereupon Andrei Gromyko, the Soviet ambassador to the United Nations, walked out. The Security Council eventually set a deadline of May 6 for the Soviets to withdraw, which they did.[28]

In August 1946, tensions flared again when the Soviets proposed to Ankara that the Montreux Convention, which gave the Turkish government sole responsibility for defending the Dardanelles or Black Sea Straits, be modified to permit a joint Turkish-Soviet defense. Truman and Churchill had agreed at Potsdam in 1945 that Montreux needed to be revised, but they had advocated that the Straits—the narrow body of water that connected the Black Sea and the Mediterranean—be an international waterway open to all and defended by all. Over a year later, however, the issue still had not been resolved. The United States interpreted the Soviets' latest proposition as another attempt to establish Soviet bases in Turkey, a step that both Turkey and the United States perceived to be a threat. In response, the administration urged Turkey to reject the Soviet offer, while the United States provided backup. The battleship *Missouri* was already at Istanbul, and now the United States sent an aircraft carrier, two cruisers, and five destroyers to the eastern Mediterranean. In addition, Under Secretary of State Dean Acheson notified the Soviet Union of the importance the United States attached to Turkey's sovereignty and sole right to defend the Straits. Navy Secretary Forrestal announced in September that the United States' presence in the eastern Mediterranean would be permanent.[29] Even as the Truman administration pursued a tougher strategy with the Soviets, though, the president still made no public comment on the Turkish situation whatsoever.

Truman certainly had approved his State Department's harder line in Iran and Turkey, but the president still had not officially split from the Soviet Union. Although he sometimes fumed behind the scenes, Truman said nothing in public. He remained ambivalent—clearly troubled, but unwilling to take a public stand. On September 6 in Stuttgart, Germany, Truman's secretary of state made news when he asserted that the United States would never allow the Soviets to control all of Germany. "As long as there is an occupation army in Germany,"

Byrnes proclaimed, "American forces will be part of that occupation army."[30] Byrnes, as the head of Truman's foreign policy, clearly spoke for the administration, but Truman himself did not speak of the new policy at all or its possible implications for U.S.-Soviet relations. In the weeks to follow, two more events occurred that would sweep the administration to greater levels of consensus on the USSR and the president closer to his ultimate decision.

Henry Wallace Controversy and Firing: September 1946

The first episode dealt, once again, with a controversial speech that Truman appeared to endorse, but this time the speaker was Henry Wallace, his secretary of commerce, who advocated a softer approach to the Soviet Union. Truman's relationship with Wallace had always been a delicate one, as Truman had replaced Wallace in the vice presidential spot on the 1944 Democratic ticket. Had Wallace remained, he would have been president instead of Truman. By September 1946, Wallace was the only New Dealer left in the cabinet so the president recognized well his value in drawing the continued support of liberal Democrats.

The two men met on September 10 and, according to Wallace's diary for that day, conferred about an address that Wallace planned to give at Madison Square Garden on September 12. Wallace recorded, "We went over it page by page, together—and again and again he said, 'That's right,' 'Yes, that is what I believe.'" At one point, according to Wallace, Truman expressed enthusiastic support for a particular line in the text: "I am neither anti-British nor pro-British—neither anti-Russian nor pro-Russian." The commerce secretary then asked the president if he could indicate that Truman supported this attitude. When Truman agreed, Wallace added a line: "And just two days ago, when President Truman read those words, he said they represented the policy of his Administration." The president, however, recalled matters differently. Truman claimed that he and Wallace had met for only fifteen minutes and had discussed the speech only in the last three. Given the time constraints, Truman said he had "tried to skim" through the text and had assumed that Wallace would not say anything that conflicted with

U.S. foreign policy. The president wrote, "One paragraph caught my eye. It said that we held no special friendship for Russia, Britain or any other country, that we wanted to see all the world at peace on an equal basis. I said that this is, of course, what we want."[31] While the two men agreed about the line that Truman had especially expressed support for, they clearly differed in regard to how much of the speech Truman had read and approved. Because Truman recorded his account after the fact on September 17, five days after Wallace delivered his controversial speech and seven days after he and Wallace first met to discuss it, his version appears the less credible.

Credibility was, in fact, what came into question on September 12 when Wallace's office distributed advance copies of the speech to the press. At the president's 4:00 P.M. news conference that day, a reporter asked whether Truman had, in fact, said that Wallace's words represented his administration's policy. Truman replied, "That is correct." When the reporter then asked if his approval applied just to that particular paragraph or to the entire speech, the president answered, "I approved the whole speech." Perhaps unable to believe what they had heard, reporters inquired further. Truman was asked if Wallace's speech was a departure from Byrnes's policy, and he breezily replied, "They are exactly in line."[32]

Chaos soon ensued, but the White House was slow to respond since—aside from the president—no one had seen the text of the address. Around 6:00 P.M., an official at the State Department found a copy lying on a distribution table at the National Press Club and quickly picked it up. Acting Secretary of State Will Clayton and Under Secretary of the Navy John Sullivan, who had gone to State to discuss the issue with Clayton, called Press Secretary Ross within the half hour to urge that Wallace be stopped. Ross thought it was too late to do so. Nonetheless, he checked with Truman, who was preparing for a poker night at Clark Clifford's. Ross recalled the president saying that the speech "might ruffle Byrnes," but "he did not think it would do any permanent damage."[33] Truman was greatly mistaken.

That evening, Wallace delivered his address before the National Citizens Political Action Committee at Madison Square Garden where an audience of twenty thousand was in attendance. White and Maze noted that the address was, in many ways, remarkably evenhanded in criticizing the individual actions of each of the major powers after the war. For example, Wallace said, "We may not like what Russia does in eastern Europe. Her type of land reform, industrial expropriation, and suppression of basic liberties offends the great majority of the United States." On the other hand, in a clear reference to recent events and ongoing tensions in the Near East, he chided that the USSR was more likely to cooperate once it understood that "our primary objective is neither saving the British Empire nor purchasing oil in the Near East with the lives of American soldiers. We must not allow national oil rivalries to force us into war."[34]

Wallace also called for cooperation between the USSR and the United States. He elaborated, "On our part, we should recognize that we have no more business in the *political* affairs of Eastern Europe than Russia has in the *political* affairs of Latin America, Western Europe, and the United States." For some critics, this line conjured up images of spheres of influence, a concept that had never found much support among Americans and which seemed at odds with Wallace's "one world" philosophy. He, however, believed that a unified world would be achieved through friendly competition between the two countries, which would result in them becoming more alike. Wallace predicted that the Soviets would be "forced to grant more and more of the personal freedoms" and the United States would become "more and more absorbed with the problems of social-economic justice." However, these points were overshadowed by his comments that repudiated the direction of White House policy. According to Wallace, "we are reckoning with a force which cannot be handled successfully by a 'Get tough with Russia' policy. 'Getting tough' never bought anything real and lasting—whether for schoolyard bullies or businessmen or world powers. The tougher we get, the tougher the Russians will get." The discovery that Wallace had cut a few passages critical of the Soviets in response to a request by organizers of the event added to the perception that he opposed Byrnes's approach and was sympathetic to the USSR.[35]

Wallace's words garnered angry reactions from all sides. His immediate audience, which had leftist predispositions, booed and hissed whenever Wallace criticized the Soviets, while newspapers ranging from the Communist Party's *Daily Worker* to the conservative *Chicago Tribune* condemned the speech. Senator Vandenberg was at the Paris Peace Conference with the secretary of state and Democratic senator Tom Connally when the news arrived, immediately prompting questions among the delegates as to whether American policy had changed. In reply, Vandenberg issued a statement to the press in which he said that most Republicans favored a bipartisan foreign policy "which rejects dictatorship by anybody, which is neither hostile nor subservient to any other power on earth and which defends human rights and fundamental freedoms." He added, in a line clearly intended for Truman, that "the situation equally requires unity within the Administration itself. We can only cooperate with one Secretary of State at a time." At home, Will Clayton openly criticized Truman's approval of the speech, and Republican senator Robert Taft of Ohio accused the president of surrendering to the left wing of the Democratic Party.[36]

Truman scrambled to find a means of escape. On September 14, the White House released a statement in which the president addressed what he called a "natural misunderstanding" about his answers to questions about Wallace's speech. In tortured prose, he explained, "It was my intention to express the thought that I approved the right of the Secretary of Commerce to deliver the speech. I did not intend to indicate that I approved the speech as constituting a statement of the foreign policy of this country." Truman insisted that "no change in the established foreign policy of our Government" had taken place. According to Clifford who, along with Ross, wrote the attempt at clarification, "Ross and I harbored a small hope that this weak and misleading statement might stop the hemorrhaging, but we were quickly brought back to reality."[37] The president's efforts to defuse the situation lacked credibility, perhaps doubly so since he had taken a similar approach in distancing himself from Churchill's speech.

To make matters worse, Wallace issued a statement of his own on September 16 in which he declared, "I stand upon my New York speech," and "I intend to continue my efforts for a just and lasting peace and I shall within the near future speak on this subject again." In Paris, Byrnes boiled with anger. From his perspective, not only was the secretary of commerce treading on his territory, but also Wallace was continuing to contradict the harder line that Byrnes had adopted. The secretary of state cabled his boss with a pointed message: "If it is not completely clear in your own mind that Mr. Wallace should be asked to refrain from criticizing the foreign policy of the United States while he is a member of your cabinet I must ask you to accept my resignation immediately." In truth, Byrnes had already told Truman that he would resign, due to health issues, as soon as the peace treaties were completed, but to have him leave earlier in response to the Wallace fiasco would have been highly embarrassing. The president and Byrnes engaged, a few days later, in a teletype "conversation," in which Truman reassured the secretary of state that he supported him and that Wallace would not be permitted to make speeches on foreign policy in the future unless they supported the administration's policy.[38]

In the meantime, the Wallace controversy continued to spiral out of control when Ross learned on September 17 that columnist Drew Pearson was about to run excerpts of a July 23 letter from Wallace to Truman that was highly critical of U.S. foreign policy. Ross swiftly conferred with Wallace and decided it was better for the entire press corps to have the letter, rather than leaving them to rely on Pearson's likely acerbic interpretations. Wallace moved to put the decision into action. When Ross consulted Truman, however, he learned that the president did not agree, but by then it was too late. Wallace maintained that someone in the State Department appeared to have leaked the letter, but years later Margaret Truman would insist—perhaps reflecting her father's views—that Wallace had leaked the letter to Pearson himself.[39]

Whatever the case, the president's patience was exhausted, and he asked Wallace to resign on September 20. Truman told the press corps, "The people of the United States may disagree freely and publicly on any question, including that of foreign policy, but the Government of the United States must stand as a unit in its relations with the rest of the world." In closing his announcement, the president underscored his support for Byrnes at the Paris Peace Conference, stating "the policies which guide him and his delegation have my full endorsement."[40]

The Wallace incident raises two questions. First, why did Wallace seek Truman's approval for a speech that would undercut Byrnes, and second, why did the president apparently give it? The answer again appears to lie with Truman's ambivalence about the way in which U.S. foreign policy was evolving. In the months leading up to his speech, Wallace had observed that Truman was capable of agreeing with contrary statements on foreign policy. Wallace recorded, for instance, that within a single hour on July 23 the president "spoke of being patient with Russia to me and then at the Cabinet luncheon agreed completely with Jimmie Byrnes in a number of cracks he took against Russia. . . . He feels completely sincere and earnest at all times and is not disturbed in the slightest by the different directions in which his mind can go almost simultaneously."[41] What Wallace may have perceived as proof of a weak intellect, however, may better be interpreted as evidence of Truman's continued struggle over how to deal with the USSR. Within his speech, the commerce secretary both criticized the Soviets and called for cooperative relations with them. Truman likely *was* attracted to Wallace's disapproval of Soviet misbehavior *and* to its Wilsonian "one world" appeals. In a conversation the two men had immediately after Wallace's speech, the commerce secretary said Truman assured him that he did not want war with the USSR and that no "get-tough-with-Russia" policy existed, while Wallace kept telling the president that "in his heart" Truman agreed with Wallace and should be wary of administration officials who were "beating the tom-toms against Russia."[42]

Wallace's efforts to seek Truman's endorsement of his speech appear, in retrospect, an attempt to obtain the president's public commitment to a different foreign policy. For his part, Truman may well have found various aspects of Wallace's message appealing, particularly since the advance text contained additional criticisms of the Soviets that Wallace had not yet deleted. Where the president demonstrated shortsightedness was in not recognizing that Wallace's message was at odds with the policy advocated by his secretary of state and, hence, with his administration's evolving foreign policy. Truman attempted to recover with his dismissal of Wallace and his statement of support for Byrnes but still did not publicly articulate a hard line toward the USSR himself. Nonetheless, the president's decision to fire Wallace had the effect of committing him more directly to the foreign policy that Wallace had disdained.

Construction and Delivery of the Clifford-Elsey Report: July–September 1946

The second episode that ultimately moved Truman along in his views also came in September of 1946, rapidly upon the heels of the first. Just four days after Wallace's resignation, the president received the Clifford-Elsey Report, an impressive-looking maroon bound volume with gold lettering that he had commissioned on July 12. Truman had inquired of Clifford if a list of agreements that the Soviets had violated could be compiled. When Clifford talked to his assistant, Elsey, about the task, Elsey recommended that a far more comprehensive study of U.S.-Soviet relations might prove more helpful. Clifford agreed, and for two months Elsey devoted himself to the project, along with his routine duties. When Clifford submitted the report to Truman on September 24, he did so under his name alone and explained that the analysis, entitled "American Relations with the Soviet Union," was based on compiled facts and studies and on consultations with "the Secretary of State, the Secretary of War, the Attorney General, the Secretary of the Navy, Fleet Admiral Leahy, the Joint Chiefs of Staff, Ambassador [Edwin] Pauley, the Director of Central Intelligence, and other persons who have special knowledge in this field."[43]

The Clifford-Elsey Report, by Clifford's own admission, drew heavily on Kennan's Long Telegram, but there were differences, as well. While Kennan had given attention both to the Soviet Union's historical situation and its current government's ideology, Clifford and Elsey discussed the USSR almost exclusively in ideological terms. The effect was largely to disregard historical factors that might help explain Soviet behavior and, instead, to attribute Soviet actions to ideology. According to the

Clifford-Elsey Report, for example, "The fundamental tenet of the communist philosophy embraced by Soviet leaders is that peaceful coexistence of communist and capitalist nations is impossible. . . . Their basic policies, domestic and foreign, are designed to strengthen the Soviet Union and to insure its victory in the predicted coming struggle between Communism and Capitalism."[44] Almost completely absent from the study were reflections on the Soviet Union's security concerns in light of its history, concerns that should have been particularly apparent so soon after World War II.

In addition, the Clifford-Elsey Report went further in its policy recommendations than Kennan. The Long Telegram had not even mentioned military strength in its conclusions about how the United States should approach the USSR, and Kennan had taken pains to emphasize that problems in U.S.-Soviet relations could be resolved without armed conflict. However, Kennan's frightening depiction of the Soviet threat, a depiction that was well received by U.S. policymakers, pointed inevitably to the need for arms—simply to defend the country, if nothing else. Clifford and Elsey depicted military strength as essential to back up the United States' words. While they asserted that the primary U.S. goal should be to convince the Soviet Union to cooperate with the rest of the world, they also argued, "The language of military power is the only language which disciples of power politics understand. The United States must use that language in order that Soviet leaders will realize that our government is determined to uphold the interests of its citizens and the rights of small nations. Compromise and concessions are considered by the Soviets, to be evidence of weakness and they are encouraged by our 'retreats' to make new and greater demands." When Truman read this passage, it may have had special salience given the ongoing Dardanelles dispute. The Clifford-Elsey Report maintained that conflict with the Soviet Union was not inevitable, but "it must be made apparent to the Soviet Government that our strength will be sufficient to repel any attack and sufficient to defeat the USSR decisively if a war should start." The analysis also advocated a more chilling military policy: "the United States must be prepared to wage atomic and biological warfare if necessary." While the report acknowledged that the actual decision to use such weapons would require "careful consideration," it maintained that the United States must be prepared in order—at the very least—to provide a compelling deterrent to Soviet actions. Likewise, Clifford and Elsey argued against all proposals for disarmament or arms limitations so long as the Soviet Union posed a threat.[45]

The Clifford-Elsey Report was noteworthy, as well, for how it forecast what would become the key principle of the Truman Doctrine. "In addition to maintaining our own strength," the study stated, "the United States should support and assist all democratic countries which are in any way menaced or endangered by the USSR. Providing military support in case of attack is a last resort; a more effective barrier to communism is strong economic support." Like the Truman Doctrine, the Clifford-Elsey Report recommended a global policy and underscored the primacy of economic assistance.[46] The importance that the report attributed to economic and other peaceful responses was easily overwhelmed, however, by its vivid portrayal of an intractable enemy and its advocacy of militarization—even extreme military measures if need be—to meet the Soviet threat.

After Truman received the analysis, he stayed up late on the evening of September 24 reading it and, promptly at 7:00 A.M. the next morning, called Clifford at home. He asked his special counsel how many copies of the report existed. "Twenty," Clifford replied. Truman then told Clifford to come quickly to the White House and give him all twenty copies before they could be distributed. According to the president, the study was very valuable, but if some of its findings became public they would "blow the roof" off the White House and the Kremlin. Clifford did as Truman asked, and the report was not heard of again until Clifford gave the final draft from which the report was printed to Arthur Krock, who published it as part of his memoirs in 1968.[47]

Although the Clifford-Elsey Report did not circulate among administration members in final form, it was an important document nonetheless. The analysis demonstrated, first of all, the degree to which a consensus was developing within the administration about the threat the USSR posed and how the United States should respond to that threat. Moreover, the process of compiling and writing the Clifford-Elsey Report helped build that consensus even more. According to Elsey, he sent letters over Clifford's signature to administration officials asking for their input. Clifford explained in the report's memo of transmittal and in subsequent interviews that the document was based on both written communication from officials and his conversations with individuals such as Marshall, Acheson, and "all of the top military leaders," a process that would have permitted the sharing—and shaping—of perceptions. At least one copy of the "last draft" of the report was shared by Clifford with Kennan, who was said to have praised it, while Leahy read portions of the report in draft form and also received a bound copy of the final version from Elsey on the same night that Clifford presented Truman with his copy.[48] One also may speculate that staff members responsible for writing their superiors' responses may have discussed the issue with one another and that cabinet-level officials, in response to Clifford's inquiries, engaged in at least informal conversation among themselves about the upcoming report and its subject matter. Taken as a whole, the very process of preparing the Clifford-Elsey Report served to reinforce and/or influence perceptions of administration officials who, in turn, had the potential to act on its premises in their communication with subordinates and each other and, hence, in their policymaking. Little wonder, then, that Clifford found "a remarkable agreement among the officials with whom I have talked and whose reports I have studied" on the grave nature of U.S.-Soviet relations and the need for a "continuous review" of U.S. policy toward the Soviet Union.[49] As noted earlier, many members of the administration had embraced the Long Telegram, and the Clifford-Elsey Report likewise drew heavily on Kennan's missive. In the insulated environment of the White House or even the State Department, shared perceptions can easily develop without challenge, a process that may have been hastened in this case by the process of formulating the Clifford-Elsey Report. Clifford made no mention of having consulted Wallace about the report and, with Truman's dismissal of his commerce secretary, the expression of divergent points of view would become even less likely in the future. If Wallace were aware of the report's ongoing construction, his knowledge of its inclinations—or assumptions about its likely contents—may explain what spurred him to gain Truman's public commitment to a different direction. Aside from its impact on other members of the administration, the Clifford-Elsey Report was significant in that it helped both Clifford and Elsey to solidify their own thinking on U.S.-Soviet relations and clearly laid the groundwork for the Truman Doctrine speech that they would play a major role in shaping.

As for Truman himself, it is harder to know what the immediate influence of the Clifford-Elsey Report was on him. He clearly recognized the volatile nature of some of its conclusions, or he would not have placed copies of the study under lock and key. Because the president had prompted the report by asking for a list of Soviet violations of international agreements, the issue of Soviet character and the degree to which he could trust Stalin was clearly on Truman's mind. It is also possible that the advocacy of military strength rang true to him, particularly when the Soviets relaxed their pressure on Turkey in October 1946, shortly after he dispatched U.S. naval power to the region. From Elsey's perspective, his work had at least some impact on the president because Truman stopped talking about offering a large loan to the Soviet Union after he read the report and recognized that its conclusions "presented the consensus of key figures in the Executive branch." However, the president still did not appear to have completely made up his mind. Only three days after Truman received the report, he wrote to former Vice Pres. John Garner that "there is too much loose talk about the Russian situation. We are not going to have any shooting trouble with them but they are tough bargainers and always ask for the whole earth, expecting maybe to get an acre."[50] In public the president also continued to refrain from speaking harsh words about the Soviets. Truman obviously read the Clifford-Elsey Report and no doubt thought about it, but the study may have exerted its greatest influence on Truman through the impact that it had on the administration policymakers who surrounded him and who participated in its construction, particularly Leahy, the joint chiefs, Byrnes, Acheson, Secretary of War Robert Patterson, Forrestal, Clifford, and Elsey. Many of these men would play significant roles in the formulation of his future foreign policy, as well as its presentation to the public.

The Stresses of Truman's Political Predicament: Fall 1946

At the time, one question that must have weighed heavily on the president's mind was the ability of the United States to provide adequate support for the policies that the Clifford-Elsey Report proposed. Americans had been anxious to shift to a peacetime footing the moment the war had ended, with women organizing a demobilization movement marked by the formation of "Bring Back Daddy" clubs and massive letter-writing campaigns. As troop levels rapidly fell through a chaotic process, administration officials like Forrestal, who were concerned about the Soviet threat, voiced worries about military readiness. Certainly, the United States had atomic supremacy at the time, but later evidence revealed that in 1947 the U.S. government had but a single atomic bomb at its disposal, a fact that further explains administration anxieties. Painter argued that even with rapid demobilization, the United States was still far stronger militarily than the Soviets for several reasons: its population had not suffered the massive number of deaths that the Soviets had during the war (thus ensuring the United States an ample supply of potential soldiers), it had a far stronger navy and air force, and the United States' capacity to support the armed forces through its agriculture and manufacturing had remained untouched. These points notwithstanding, the Soviet Union had far more troops than the United States by the end of 1946, many of which were concentrated in or near vulnerable regions of interest to U.S. policymakers—Europe and the Near East—thereby enhancing American officials' perceptions of threat. Gen. George C. Marshall, who replaced Byrnes as secretary of state in January 1947, shed light on such concerns when he later recalled his bargaining position at the Moscow summit of March 1947. According to Marshall, he received a great deal of urging to "give the Russians hell" in Moscow, but "my facilities for giving them hell . . . was 1–1/3 divisions over the entire United States. This is quite a proposition when you deal with somebody with over 260 and you have 1–1/3."[51]

As the United States transitioned to peacetime, Harry Truman not only had the Soviets and demobilization to consider but also the struggling economy. Business no longer wanted price controls and waged a bitter campaign on the Office of Price Administration (OPA). With the assistance of a cooperative Congress, business succeeded in getting passage of legislation that continued the OPA in name but stripped it of its authority. Truman vetoed the legislation, which had the effect of lifting price controls until he could sign a subsequent bill. As a result, prices rose rapidly, a meat shortage developed, and the new law that the president approved did little more to help the OPA control prices than the previous bill had. Truman resigned himself to the situation and lifted most price controls entirely on October 14, 1946. When it came to labor, the president fared no better. Unions wanted wage controls removed once the war was over, particularly as prices rose. In 1946 alone, autoworkers, steelworkers, railroad workers, and coal miners all went on strike, wreaking havoc on the economy and requiring that Truman himself get personally involved in the disputes.[52] This plethora of economic problems encouraged Americans to look inward even more, rather than concern themselves with matters of the larger world, a fact that the president surely recognized. Unfortunately for Truman, the American people also blamed him for their troubles.

By the fall of 1946, Truman's popular support had gone from 82 percent to 32 percent in just a year. Domestic problems had taken their toll on him. In addition, his handling of the Churchill and Wallace speeches had made him appear incompetent or deceitful or both. Those on the left believed the Truman administration's foreign policy had embarked on a dangerous course, whereas those on the right, exploiting the president's refusal to break formally with the Soviets, charged that the administration was too soft. The situation had become so dire that Democratic leaders asked Truman not to campaign for the party's candidates in the last few weeks before the midterm elections, but it made no difference. In November, the New Deal officially left power when Republicans won control of the House by a margin of 246 to 188 and the Senate by 51 to 45. It was a humiliating blow. As Truman's train pulled into Washington, D.C., from Independence the next day, only Acheson stood waiting on the platform to greet him.[53]

Privately, the administration worried that the new Congress would be as focused on domestic issues as most of the nation's citizens were and try to cut the defense budget, occupation appropriations, and foreign aid. Their worries were well founded. As a *New York Times* editorial explained it, the budget allocated for international affairs and foreign aid was alluring to isolationist Republicans because its $3.5 billion in expenses could "become three and half billions nestling snugly in the pockets of politically grateful American taxpayers."[54] Truman, still personally torn between his commitment to Wilsonian ideals and his increasing concerns over Soviet behavior, now headed an administration unified by its consensus that a hard line was needed. Simultaneously, the president had to contend with continuing citizen disinterest in world affairs, his own low standing, and an incoming Congress that was likely to obstruct his every move. The pressure must have been enormous.

Stress had plagued Truman much of his adult life, with recurrent headaches starting during his young political career back in Kansas City in the 1920s. Truman had checked himself into hospitals several times when he was in the Senate—often at Bess's insistence—after suffering from headaches, nausea, and exhaustion. In 1937, doctors at the Army Hospital in Hot Springs, Arkansas, concluded that Truman was suffering from stress compounded by overwork and physical inactivity. The senator began walking and swimming almost daily, a habit that would continue when he entered the White House. In April 1943, Bess had again insisted that he go to the Army Hospital in Hot Springs for a round of examinations, which revealed that he had an acidic stomach from pushing himself too hard.[55]

In the White House, Dr. Wallace Graham became Truman's personal physician, and he quickly noticed that stress continued to affect the president. Graham later revealed that whenever Truman got tense, his lungs produced more fluid than usual, particularly in the early years of his presidency during such episodes as when the Soviets initially refused to leave Iran in March 1946. According to the physician, he gave Truman diuretics when he needed them and reminded him, "'You know, you're captain of your own ship, Mr. President.'" Truman poked fun at himself, calling the fluid build-up in his lungs "an old ladies' reaction" or complaint, but agreed that he needed to take steps to alleviate his tension. In addition to his daily exercise, Truman distracted himself with poker games, long weekends on the *Williamsburg*, and frequent visits to Key West. By November 1946, the president had spent a year and a half trying to come to terms with U.S.-Soviet relations and grappling with the postwar transition at home, only to find himself renounced and the party he led trounced in the midterm elections. It was enough to cause anyone anxiety, let alone Truman, who was prone to stress anyway. Not surprisingly, he left for Key West to escape shortly after the election and, in a letter to Bess, wrote in sheer frustration, "I'm doing as I damn please for the next two years and to hell with all of them."[56]

Truman did not really mean it, of course, for he had too much personal ambition and too much selfless patriotism to ignore his critics completely. Undoubtedly, Truman hoped the coming year would be better. Back in Washington, D.C., in December, he briefly met with a man whose country would, in a few short months, be at the center of the president's decision to change the course of U.S. foreign policy and, hence, the course of the Truman administration and the world. This turning point would also demonstrate the power of rhetoric to shape perceptions of policymakers in the administration, including President Truman himself.

U.S. Lack of Urgency Regarding Greece: December 1946–February 1947

Constantine Tsaldaris, the prime minister of Greece, had come to the United States in December 1946 for two reasons. First, he publicly asked the United Nations to investigate guerilla activity occurring in Greece along its shared border with Albania, Yugoslavia, and Bulgaria, a request the United Nations approved over the objections of the USSR and Poland. Second, Tsaldaris privately asked the United States for aid. For years, the British had supported the Greek government that was now immersed in a civil war, but British Foreign Minister Bevin encouraged Tsaldaris to turn to the United States for future assistance and said, "If you go, I am going to help you." The U.S. State Department did not welcome the prime minister with open arms. According to Acheson, Tsaldaris was "a weak, pleasant, but silly man" who asked the United States for billions of dollars in aid. Mark Ethridge, who served as a U.S. delegate on the U.N. Commission to Greece, would later describe the prime minister in blunter terms. "Tsaldaris was a stupid fool" and, he said, the diplomatic community who dealt with Tsaldaris shared that opinion.[57]

Despite their personal assessment of Tsaldaris, the Americans recognized the importance of Greece as well as its precarious situation. The British government had begun asking the United States to join in its assistance efforts as early as December 1945, and the United States had sent several hundred American personnel to oversee the Greek election after the war. The United States had also assisted the Greek government in securing a $25 million loan from the Import-Export Bank. Furthermore, Truman himself had great affection for Greece. After examining Acheson's letter informing the Greeks of the loan and warning them to adopt economic reforms or risk future assistance, the president critiqued his under secretary of state's typically brusque style. Truman wrote that he found the note "rather harsh, in view of the fact that the Greeks were almost annihilated fighting our common enemy, the Germans, and while they have had some severe internal difficulty with the British, I can't help but feel extremely friendly to the Greeks. . . . . [C]an't we say the same things and implement the same policy in a little more friendly way." Regardless of any warmth Truman felt for Greece, however, Tsaldaris left his brief December 20, 1946, meeting with the president with no definitive offer of aid. Undaunted, the prime minister announced upon his return to Greece that an American loan would be forthcoming. Secretary of State Byrnes quickly informed the British ambassador, Lord Inverchapel, however, that no such commitment had been made, but that the United States could not "stop Tsaldaris from making a statement he believes will be helpful to him at home."[58]

American officials had reason to hesitate, for the situation in Greece was a mess. Even before World War II hostilities had ended, the country had erupted into a civil war that involved several different groups. The EAM, the National Liberation Front, was a coalition of resistance groups formed in September 1941 that included the Greek Communists, or KKE. In 1942, EAM formed the National People's Liberation Army or ELAS, which managed to attract a wide range of individuals, from KKE members to Greek military officers. The second-largest resistance group was the National Republican Greek League, or EDES, that was anti-Communist in character and gradually became more monarchical and conservative, as well, eventually leading some of its units to collaborate with the Nazis against the ELAS. In addition, Security Battalions, who got their funding from the Germans, were strongly motivated by anti-Communism and also fought against ELAS. The various resistance groups began turning their weapons on each other at the end of 1943, but the civil war was not one fought purely on a class or ideological basis. In 1944, for example, ELAS defeated the National Social Liberation group, or EKKA, but some of EKKA's remaining members joined the Nazis and the Security Battalions, while others became members of ELAS. Personal factors such as family ties, desire for revenge, need for economic security, and promise of plunder often exerted their influence as much as ideology did.[59]

Regardless of their motives, all of the groups engaged in horrific atrocities against civilians, with the mayhem continuing after the Nazis had been defeated and the Greek government-in-exile had returned. U.S. intelligence at the start of 1947 believed that KKE bands were carrying out most of the attacks on the government but that EAM, also dominated by Communists and of which KKE was a part, was engaged in guerrilla warfare along the border of Yugoslavia and possibly Albania and Bulgaria, as well. Yugoslavia, U.S. intelligence believed, was training and equipping the EAM fighters, but there were "indications that this fighting in Greece is part of a Soviet-inspired plan to dominate all of the Balkans." Meanwhile, domestic politics in Greece were completely polarized, particularly when the highly controversial king was permitted to return to Greece. Secretary of State Marshall, new on the job in January 1947, articulated the problem quite well in a telegram to the U.S. embassy in Greece: "Many former adherents of liberal and center parties, alarmed at presence of communists or condonement of communism, seem to have gravitated towards extreme right while others shocked at reactionary attitude of rightists have gone over to groups controlled or contaminated by communists." The only way the situation could be remedied, Marshall advised the embassy, was if "responsible Greek political leaders would have the vision, restraint, and patriotism" to form a political coalition that rejected both the extreme left and the extreme right.[60] Unfortunately, such vision, restraint, and patriotism were in short supply.

American officials also were wary of giving money to a corrupt government that consistently refused to adopt economic reforms that would, in the long run, help Greece to recover from the war and stabilize the political situation. On the day of Tsaldaris's meeting with Truman, a memorandum providing background information on Greece for Treasury Secretary John Snyder noted that the Greek government had frivolously squandered its gold and foreign exchange reserves for short-term gain. The poor state of the Greek economy was due not only to "political instability and strife" but also to "Greek Government ineptness and lack of courage in the economic and financial fields." When it came to serving citizen needs, Paul A. Porter, who headed the American Economic Mission to Greece, found the government equally lacking. He pondered, on February 1, 1947, as he visited Greece, "How can a representative democracy hope to function when it is organized from the top down? There is no pressure the people can exert for such fundamental things as road improvements and basic reconstruction."[61]

The Americans had also hesitated to get involved in Greece because it was considered to be Britain's problem. In the fall of 1944, Churchill had met with Stalin in Moscow because of his concerns over the westward progress of the Soviet army and what this would ultimately mean for the countries that the Soviets occupied. President Roosevelt, busy with the upcoming election, dispatched Harriman as his representative. Before Harriman could reach Moscow, however, Churchill and Stalin quietly made an agreement that gave the USSR dominance in Rumania and Bulgaria—countries the Soviets already occupied—and the British dominance in Greece. In December 1944, the British would rely upon that agreement when it used force to bring down an EAM-ELAS uprising in post-occupation Athens. The United States, of course, had always rejected "spheres of influence" not only on principle, but also because its citizenry came from a variety of ethnic backgrounds, thereby ensuring that some segment of the public would always oppose such a policy. Nevertheless, once Roosevelt and then Truman learned of the British-Soviet agreement, they recognized that a benefit to the arrangement was that it relieved Washington of responsibility. As a Treasury Department memorandum noted in December 1946, "The United States Government has not taken an active role in Greece's internal affairs since Greece is considered to be in the British sphere of influence." This point was not lost on the British. In the spring of 1945, Lord Halifax had observed that the United States had no interest in involving itself in Greece "so long as His Majesty's Government continues to be willing to keep the initiative," a state of affairs that was quite acceptable to Great Britain until the strain on its own coffers became too much.[62]

Still, if U.S. officials had wanted to provide Greece with further aid, each of these reasons for hesitation would immediately have become problems of rhetorical strategy, as well. The Republican Congress, still dominated by isolationists, would have been loath to provide foreign aid of any kind, as would most American citizens of the time. And even if they had agreed with the White House that the United States should aid endangered democracies, many members of Congress and the citizenry at large would have asked, Why help the corrupt, incompetent, and possibly pro-fascist government of Greece, and why help the British with their colonial undertakings? Indeed, when the Truman administration did decide to intervene in March 1947, these questions became issues that the administration had to grapple with as it prepared the president's message to Congress.

In the context of late 1946 to early 1947, however, the Truman administration was still happy to defer action. Acheson urged the U.S. ambassadors in both Greece and Turkey in November 1946 to discourage the governments there from asking the United States for military equipment and to encourage them to go to the British instead. Although Soviet actions in regard to Iran and Turkey had raised U.S. concerns, U.S. intelligence could not definitively say that the USSR was behind guerrilla activity in Greece, and a number of officials thought the Greek government exaggerated its problems, which also may have dampened U.S. enthusiasm for providing additional Greek aid. Washington helped in relatively small ways, such as providing Greece with eight C-47s and supporting Tsaldaris's request at the United Nations. Nonetheless, these were half-hearted efforts. The United States had promised to send an economic mission to Greece in October 1946 but waited to name a director, Paul A. Porter, for several months. According to Porter, he and the administration both knew that the mission was "a delaying tactic, not a prelude to significant new American aid."[63] Great Britain, however, would soon force the United States' hand because, if Greek aid were to continue, there was no other choice.

British Notes Arrive at State: February 21, 1947

After emerging victorious from the war, Great Britain was, ironically enough, brought to its knees by the weather when one of the worst winters in history began battering much of Europe in January 1947. Bitter temperatures, heavy snowfalls, and driving winds brought transportation to a standstill, further devastating Britain's already-crippled economy. By February, the government had to cut off electricity to manufacturers in several regions and close down electric service five hours each day to households. Millions of people were unemployed. To manage what he called "an emergency of the utmost gravity," Prime Minister Clement Attlee and his government rapidly spent funds, leaving reserves dangerously low. He and his cabinet, faced with the realities of the nation's economic situation, came to the conclusion that Great Britain must significantly trim its foreign expenses, a decision that led to independence for Burma and India. Moreover, the British decided that they could no longer afford to support the Greek government, nor to send aid to the Turks.[64]

Accordingly, the British embassy contacted the State Department on

Friday, February 21, with messages for the secretary of state. Marshall, however, had left town to prepare for a speech at Princeton University the next day, a speech in which he would encourage Americans to develop "a sense of responsibility for world order and security." As a courtesy, the British embassy presented Loy Henderson, the director of Near Eastern and African Affairs, with copies of two notes, the originals of which the ambassador would present formally to Marshall the following Monday. The notes informed the Americans that Britain's economic problems would force the Attlee government to discontinue all aid to Greece and Turkey, effective March 31, and encouraged the United States to assume the responsibility. After reading the notes, Henderson and Jack Hickerson, the director of European Affairs, brought them to Acheson. The under secretary of state looked at the notes and then, according to Henderson, directed him to "get your staff together and work like hell over this weekend." Acheson said he wanted the staff to write a memorandum on the matter that Acheson could give to Marshall early Monday before his 10:00 A.M. meeting with Lord Inverchapel. Later, Acheson would recall that the British notes were "shockers."[65]

The administration's sense of urgency, on the surface, seems odd since the White House had said very little about Greece publicly and had done relatively little to help it. Behind the scenes, American diplomats initially sent reports that described Greece as troubled both financially and politically, but these reports would become more emotional and urgent in tone over time. The U.S. ambassador to Greece, Lincoln MacVeagh, sent messages on February 7 and February 11 that argued he had no expectation of direct Russian military or political intervention in Greece but that dismal economic conditions—conditions that Porter dispassionately detailed for the administration in a report on February 17—might "soon cause revolution on a nationwide scale which the well organized Communist party [in Greece] can be counted on to dominate if not openly lead." He also agreed with the U.N.'s conclusions that the KKE was receiving help from the Communist parties that controlled Greece's Balkan neighbors.[66] MacVeagh seemed to describe a situation that was troubled but not dire.

By contrast, Ethridge, the U.S. representative on the U.N. Commission to Greece, conveyed a far more critical scene when, on February 17—the same day as Porter's matter-of-fact report—he sent to Marshall a message of escalated urgency that directly implicated the Soviets. Ethridge warned, "the Soviets feel that Greece is a ripe plum ready to fall into their hands within a few weeks" and that if Greece fell, then Italy and France would quickly follow. According to Ethridge, the U.N. commissioners with whom he served "feel that after having been rebuffed in Azerbaijan and Turkey [the] Soviets are finding Greece surprisingly soft and that matter has gone beyond probing [the] state and is now an all out offensive for the kill." He concluded, "Urgently suggest that matter has reached necessity for highest level consideration and action involving coordination with Britain." In response, Marshall telegrammed the U.S. embassy in Greece on February 18 to encourage MacVeagh to confer with Porter and Ethridge on the matter; meanwhile, he said he was sending Ethridge's assessment to the U.S. embassy in London to gain their perspective on the situation.[67]

The very next day, the *charge d'affaires* in London, Waldemar Gallman, reported to Marshall, "British sources in Greece do not confirm [the] seriousness of internal Greek position as presented by Ethridge." Gallman said neither the British embassy in Greece, nor Richard Windle who served with Ethridge on the U.N. Commission, believed that Greece was about to fall to Communism. Rather, Gallman argued, the U.N. Commission's presence had led to a decrease in help from abroad for the Greek Communists. He did, however, agree that the economic situation in Greece was serious and that "*if* allowed to deteriorate and to result in a collapse, would precipitate a grave political situation, which in turn *might* lead to Communist rule" (emphasis added). In short, then, the British did not perceive Greece to be on the brink of disaster, as Ethridge did. Nor did Turkey appear to be under immediate threat. As noted earlier, the Russians had relaxed their pressure on Turkey since October, a point that Marshall observed during the meeting with Lord Inverchapel on February 24 when he received the British notes. In sum, uniform consensus on the status of Greece did not appear to exist. And while the United States continued to have concerns about the long-term security of Turkey, the Soviets had taken no additional action in five months.[68] Why, then, did the Truman administration treat the situation in Greece and, to a lesser degree, Turkey as a major crisis once the British made their intentions known?

One possible explanation, in line with Acheson's "shockers" comment, is that American officials were not prepared for the British decision and, when it came, they were taken by surprise. According to Clifford, however, the British move was not sudden, but rather British officials had sent informal word of the impending withdrawal several times in late 1946. Certainly Tsaldaris's personal plea to the president in December was a signal of what was to come. In his memoirs, Truman wrote, "the crisis came sooner than we expected," a statement that suggests he knew the British were going to pull out of Greece and Turkey.[69] Perhaps Acheson, Truman, and other members of the administration were simply too preoccupied with other issues they faced, particularly on the heels of a devastating election, to recognize the extent of Britain's problems. Clearly, though, they should not have been surprised.

Another explanation for why the administration treated Greece as such a crisis lies, to a large degree, with Dean Acheson and with the power of rhetoric—even policy rhetoric assumed to be objective in nature—to influence perceptions. When Marshall became secretary of state on January 21, 1947, he convinced Acheson to defer his decision to leave the department and resume his law practice until June 30. Acheson, who would eventually become Truman's secretary of state himself, found his role much improved under Marshall's leadership. From the start, Marshall made it clear that he wanted the under secretary to act as a chief of staff and run the department. Questions and issues that arose were to go to Acheson first and then to Marshall.[70] In practical terms, this meant that Dean Acheson had a great deal more power to decide which issues went to the secretary of state—and to shape the discussion of those issues—than he had in the past.

The relevance of this organizational change to Greece is significant. On the same day—February 19—that Gallman sent his telegram disputing Ethridge's assessment, Porter sent a personal telegram to Ben Cohen, the counselor for the Department of State and, as Acheson described him, "my old friend." Porter pleaded with Cohen that "Nature of crisis here such that I urge you [to] recommend strongly to Secretary [that] he come to Greece enroute to Moscow [conference]" to demonstrate support for Greece, a course of action that Ethridge and MacVeagh had already suggested. According to Porter, "I would not make this personal appeal to you in absence of well considered conviction developments here [in] next few months could determine the future." Porter asked Cohen to make the appeal to Marshall, but surely Porter also knew that such an appeal would first go through Cohen's good friend, Dean Acheson. Although Porter's suggestion was not acted upon, Cohen telegrammed him on February 21 that his suggestion "was thoroughly and sympathetically considered yesterday by top policy committee. Unfortunately such visit impossible before Moscow." Marshall may not have gone to Greece, but Porter did have his case heard, both by the under secretary and the secretary, as well as other members of the "top policy committee" within State. On February 20, MacVeagh reinforced Porter's perspectives when he sent another telegram for Marshall, per the secretary of state's inquiry, that stated he, Porter, and Ethridge were in agreement about the "critical" status of Greece.[71] Whether the situation in Greece had deteriorated drastically or Porter and MacVeagh had been influenced by Ethridge's interpretation of events is hard to say, but their messages depicted Greece's status as far more dangerous than Gallman and British officials in Greece had a mere day before.

In addition to messages coming from Greece, Acheson encountered internal messages that urged action, again from an old friend. Henderson had long argued for a hard line with the Soviets, a point of view that was unpopular in State during the war but that also explains why he received Kennan's Long Telegram so favorably. After World War II concluded, Henderson tried, without success, to get State Department officers interested in a more significant American role in the Near East. Eventually, his arguments won over Acheson, whom he had known for years and with whom he had a very close relationship. On February 20, the day before the British notes arrived, Henderson submitted a memorandum to Acheson entitled "Critical Situation in Greece." Acheson read it, reordered its points a bit, added the telegrams from MacVeagh, Porter, and Ethridge as an appendix, and then gave the report a new title that was far more ominous: "Crisis and Imminent Possibility of Collapse in Greece."[72] The title change may have been a strategic choice intended to persuade the secretary, or it may simply have represented, in Acheson's view, a more accurate description. Regardless, rhetoric was at work.

In the memorandum, the language of Acheson's new title, as well as the prose of the report itself, promoted a sense of crisis. "Unless urgent and immediate support is given to Greece," the memorandum warned, "it seems probable that the Greek Government will be overthrown and a totalitarian regime of the extreme left will come to power." Acheson and Henderson also clarified that it was not just a Communist government in Greece that the United States had to fear but "Soviet domination" of Greece that, in turn, might "result in the loss of the whole Near and Middle East and northern Africa." Based on these assumptions, the memorandum called for the internal reform of the Greek government and for economic and military aid from Great Britain and the United States. More specifically, Acheson and Henderson argued, "If we are to act at all, we recommend presenting a special bill to Congress on an urgent basis for a direct loan to Greece, stressing the fact that if inflation and chaos are not prevented within the next few months, the gravest consequences will ensue and the country will be beyond our help." The introductory phrase of this sentence—"If we are to act at all"—acknowledged that the secretary and the president had not yet decided to provide Greece with further assistance, but its crisis language, along with the urgency of the attached telegrams, clearly attempted to shift the burden of proof. In his memoirs, Acheson would recall that he had given the memorandum to Marshall on February 20 and that the secretary of state had, in turn, told him to "prepare the necessary steps for sending economic aid" before departing for Princeton the next day. This does not appear to be the case, however, for the memo itself is dated February 21, and Marshall's itinerary for his Princeton trip on February 21 indicates that he was picked up at 7:30 A.M. at his residence and taken directly to Union Station.[73] Instead, in all likelihood, Acheson had the memorandum waiting for the secretary upon his return.

The same day that Acheson edited Henderson's memo, another telegram from Ethridge arrived that again urged action in Greece and claimed that his own discussions with fellow U.N. commissioners and British, Greek, and American military personnel supported his views, rather than those conveyed by Gallman.[74] Later that afternoon, the British embassy delivered copies of the diplomatic notes on Greece and Turkey to Henderson and Hickerson. The secretary of state was out of town, and Dean Acheson was in charge.

In accordance with Acheson's request, Henderson, Hickerson, and key staff members worked all weekend preparing a second memorandum that summarized the facts of the situation, funds and personnel needed to help Greece and Turkey, the funds and personnel that were already available, the strategic importance of Greece and Turkey to Western Europe, and, most important of all, actions that should be taken. Henderson and Hickerson also asked Kennan, who was then at the War College in Washington, D.C., to chair one meeting since Marshall had recently appointed him to create and direct a policy planning staff, an appointment that would begin in May. After discussing the issue with the others, Kennan agreed with them that the United States needed to give generous aid to Greece, but Turkey was barely discussed. Henderson and Hickerson also conferred that weekend with Vice Adm. Forrest Sherman, deputy chief of naval operations, and Maj. Gen. Lauris Norstad, director of plans and operations of the War Department general staff. For his part, Acheson telephoned Truman and Marshall and told them "what had happened, what had been done, and asked for further orders. They had none."[75]

On Sunday morning, Henderson brought the final draft of the proposal to Acheson at his Georgetown home. Henderson also asked if the group's focus was now on making the decision of whether to extend aid to Greece and Turkey or implementing that decision. Acheson later wrote, "I told him the latter; under the circumstances, there could be only one decision." They drank martinis to celebrate. Indeed, Henderson told an interviewer in 1973, "I had not been surprised when Mr. Acheson had approved our memorandum of action. He and I had been discussing the problems of Greece and Turkey for some time, and both of us felt a crisis with regard to them was imminent."[76] With Acheson and Henderson at the helm in Marshall's absence, any policy other than extending aid to Greece and Turkey seems unfathomable. The organizational structure established by Marshall and the personal relationships of Acheson virtually ensured that State Department officials advocating on behalf of aid to Greece would have their pleas heard. Moreover, the urgent language of Ethridge found its way into Acheson's own arguments, thereby heightening the perceived importance of Greek aid.

This is *not* to say that Marshall would have decided against extending aid to Greece if Acheson were not there. In his own messages of the time, the secretary of state made clear that he perceived Soviet Communism to be a threat, but he was not as alarmist as Ethridge and Acheson were. His telegram to MacVeagh, after receiving Ethridge's February 17 message, stated: "Dept. discussing with Brit Emb here. Hope you can talk over situation immediately with Ethridge and Porter and inform Dept of your concerted views as to seriousness of situation and, if collapse seems probable and immediate, how much time remains for any remedial action which US or UK might take."[77] While the secretary of state perceived a Soviet threat, he tended to be more matter of fact and deliberate in how he talked about the situation in Greece. Acheson, by contrast, discussed Greece as a major crisis, thereby heightening its importance and increasing the urgency of making a decision quickly.

And then there was Truman. With an allegiance to Wilsonian cooperation and also an underlying belief in the primacy of power, the president had attended to Stalin's 1946 election-eve speech with little alarm but had listened with increasing concern to Churchill's Fulton address and to members of his administration who had embraced the Long Telegram as they discussed a gradually hardening line with the Soviets. In September 1946, Truman had fired the major dissenting voice in his administration and, a few days later, read a deeply disturbing document, the Clifford-Elsey Report, that argued economic assistance to other countries, a strengthened military at home, and even a willingness to engage in atomic and biological warfare might be needed to counter the threat that the Soviets posed. All of these events served, in different ways, to construct a rhetorical framework through which to interpret Soviet acts in regard to Iran and Turkey, a framework that the State Department and a number of other administration officials readily adopted.

At the same time, alternative frameworks might have provided more complex interpretations. Stalin was a brutal dictator, but in Iran it was also true that the Iranians had played the Americans against the Soviets and that the Iranian government had clearly favored the Americans in its negotiations for oil concessions. While American officials pointed to Bulgaria and Rumania, they ignored the Soviets' decisions to permit non-Communist governments in Finland and Hungary—the latter only until after the Truman Doctrine—and assumed, wrongly, that Yugoslavia under Tito and its support for the KKE were directly controlled by Moscow. Ideology pulled the Soviet government, but so did its historic insecurities, insecurities rooted in past events that motivated the Soviet desire to control the Black Sea Straits. From their perspective, the Soviets may have seen their domination of Poland and Bulgaria as no different than Churchill's use of British troops against the leftist resistance in Greece in December 1944 or his attempt to keep Carlo Sforza out of the government in Italy.[78]

Conclusion

While the history of world war and the president's intimate knowledge of Wilson's writing led him to support cooperative relations with the Soviets and the formation of the United Nations, he puzzled over how to interpret Soviet actions. Over time, the rhetoric of Kennan, Churchill, Clifford and Elsey, and others shaped an increasingly narrow interpretive framework through which administration officials viewed Soviet behavior, a framework that played on Truman's beliefs about power. The president's long public silence on the matter also created, in Medhurst's words, a "rhetorical vacuum," which opposing politicians were happy to fill. In January 1947, for instance, Republican Everett Dirksen rose on the floor of the House to warn his colleagues about Communist expansion abroad. He spoke of the "virus" of Communism, "red fever," and the "plague" of what he termed "red fascism."

In a similar fashion, Sen. Styles Bridges of New Hampshire attacked the Democrats that same month for their "sorry mess of appeasement and political muddling" during the war years. Hinds and Windt argued that the United States had a history of anti-Communism that, as the Cold War began, provided a rich rhetorical stockpile of language and imagery upon which anti-Communists could draw. Moreover, the polarized language used to assail fascism during World War II was easily converted to attack Communism.[79]

The messages that Truman encountered—both within his administration and without—gradually narrowed the president's perceptions until, in February 1947, he accepted the messages' framework as his own. Once he did so, the president had no second thoughts. Truman himself may have explained his thought process best when he wrote to Eleanor Roosevelt, "The Greek-Turkish matter which you mentioned has, I think, caused me more worry and soul-searching than any matter in these past two years. I felt the grave responsibility of the decision and the drawbacks to any course of action suggested. But it has also brought me, when the decision was made and as the issues have developed here and abroad, a growing feeling of certainty in the rightness of our step."[80]

When Acheson called to tell the president about the British notes, Clifford was with Truman. Clifford recalled, "It was clear from listening to the President's end of the conversation that he was prepared for suggestions from Acheson to offer Greece and Turkey substantial aid." Given the framework repeatedly presented to him, Truman could no longer ignore the political power implications of the Greek situation nor the Soviet culprit who appeared to be responsible. Upon his return from Princeton, Marshall studied the two memoranda that Acheson had waiting for him and then discussed them with Truman, who approved their recommendations. Hence, Acheson's revision of the one report and direction of the other's preparation further reinforced the perception that Greece constituted a crisis. It was a role he would continue to play in the weeks to come when Marshall delegated the Greek-Turkish problem to his under secretary as Marshall prepared for the Moscow foreign ministers conference.[81]

In examining Truman's conclusion that Greece was a crisis instigated by the Soviets, the credibility of his secretary of state also undoubtedly played a role. George Marshall's public stature at the time he became secretary of state rivaled that of Gen. George Washington in his own time. For his part, Truman worshipped Marshall, writing on his appointments sheet for February 18, 1947, after a meeting with his secretary of state, "The more I see and talk to him the more certain I am he's the great one of the age. I am surely lucky to have his friendship and support." As for Marshall, he sensed the president's complete trust in him, as well, but felt uncomfortable with it. Marshall told historian Forrest Pogue in 1956 that Truman's faith in the secretary of state had "always frightened me. . . . I could get him to approve anything, but I knew enough to know I didn't have the whole field [might not understand everything I should about a situation]."[82] The fact that Marshall presented and endorsed the arguments that Acheson had prepared made it all the easier for Truman to forge ahead with a new foreign policy.

In the weeks that followed, the rhetoric of the past—and the reality it had generated—continued to shape the administration's perceptions as officials began work on a persuasive campaign to win congressional and public support for aid to Greece and Turkey.

CHAPTER 3

The Campaign Begins

Advance Work of Congressional Consultation and News Management

On Sunday, March 9, Special Counsel Clark Clifford and his assistant, George Elsey, met to begin editing the State Department's draft of the president's upcoming speech on Greece and Turkey. Clifford turned to Elsey and declared that the address would be "the opening gun in a campaign to bring people up to the realization that the war isn't over by any means."[1] Clifford, however, was wrong, for the campaign had already begun in the form of advance work with leaders of Congress and members of the press in order to prepare the way for the president's speech.

To understand this early campaign work, one has to go back to the memorandum prepared at the State Department on the weekend that the British notes arrived. It provided background and possible responses. In addition, the document stated that the Eightieth Congress was unlikely to vote for legislation providing aid unless its members understood how serious the situation was and believed the policy had public support. As a result, Henderson explained, the officers proposed to Marshall three key steps:

1. Convince the president of the importance of extending aid and of proposing that Congress pass the necessary legislation.

2. Suggest that the president be armed with documents that could convince key members of Congress whom he would call into a conference of the necessity for such legislation.

3. That in order to gain popular support the president make a speech to the country in which for the first time since the war he would tell the people of the United States of the dangers to the free world arising from the aggressiveness and expansionism of international communism.[2]

The memorandum—approved by Acheson, then Marshall, and then Truman—sparked additional attention to the need for persuasion in the days ahead.

On Monday, February 24, after Marshall had met with the British foreign secretary and discussed the situation with the president, he left for the *USS Williamsburg* where the weekly cabinet luncheon was to be held. Marshall caught Navy Secretary Forrestal just prior to the luncheon, showing him the State Department memorandum and reviewing the contemplated action. After the meal, Truman and Marshall met in Acheson's office with Forrestal, Secretary of War Patterson, Admiral Sherman, General Norstad, Henderson, Hickerson, and Acheson to discuss events in the Near East. It soon became clear to Acheson that "the President and his principal advisers seemed convinced that it was vital to the security of the United States for Greece and Turkey to be strengthened to preserve their national independence, that only the United States could do this, that funds and authority from Congress were necessary, and that State would prepare for concurrence by War and Navy specific recommendations for the President." In turn, Acheson, Henderson, and other State Department personnel got to work, again paying attention to the need to win public support for the new policy.[3]

The State Department's Turn to Public Affairs

The State Department's attention to what it termed "public affairs" had grown during World War II. In addition to the usual press releases and publications, State Department officials gave occasional speeches, but these endeavors were not extensive. The department intensified its efforts in the middle of the war, however, by expanding its publications that summarized news and interpreted world affairs for U.S. diplomats abroad. In addition, State began a new publication in October 1943, *Bulletin of the Department of State,* which included articles, primary documents, and speech texts intended for public consumption. The department's attempts at public outreach intensified when Secretary of State Cordell Hull became troubled over conversations he had with representatives from private organizations like chambers of commerce, the League of Women Voters, and labor organizations who were frustrated that there was no place at the State Department where they could get additional information or share their views. On June 29, 1943, Hull appointed John Dickey to create a program that would establish better relations between State and private groups. Dickey initiated a radio series, *The State Department Speaks,* in January 1944 in which a number of top-ranking officials, including then Assistant Secretary of State Dean Acheson, took part. During that same month, Hull reorganized the State Department to create the Office of Public Information, with Dickey as its director. The intention of the office was to keep citizens and Congress informed about U.S. foreign policy. With the reorganization, the Office of Public Information included not only the established divisions of Current Information and Research and Publications but also the new Motion Picture and Radio Division and Division of Science, Education, and Art. Dickey then created the Division of Public Liaison in February 1944 with several goals in mind: to provide speakers and information to private groups, to collect and study data relating to public opinion on foreign policy matters, and to manage correspondence with citizens about U.S. foreign policy.[4]

By December of that year, Hull had resigned due to health reasons, and Edward Stettinius became the new secretary of state. He immediately approved one of several reorganization plans presented to him that modified the January 1944 changes. Under the new structure, Archibald MacLeish became assistant secretary of state for public and cultural relations, a designation that further underscored the new importance that the department attached to public relations efforts, and Dickey served as director of the renamed Office of Public Affairs under him. The reorganization brought greater departmental attention to overseas communication but, more germane to the campaign to win public acceptance for aid to Greece and Turkey, it placed a special focus on domestic programs. For example, MacLeish arranged seven radio broadcasts on topics such as "America's Foreign Policy," "What about the Enemy Countries?," and "It's Your State Department," to which the public feedback was overwhelmingly positive. When MacLeish resigned in 1945, Truman appointed William Benton, the vice president of the University of Chicago who once headed an advertising agency. Dickey left the same year to become president of Dartmouth, and his friend, Francis Russell, whom he had brought to State, replaced him as director of the Office of Public Affairs.[5]

Under the direction of Russell, the Office of Public Affairs engaged in a number of activities. Its Division of Public Opinion Research conducted surveys and subscribed to major periodicals and one hundred U.S. newspapers. In addition, the division provided, to State Department policy officers, reports on public opinion trends gleaned from newspaper editorials, surveys, and the mail. The Division of Publications continued to create summaries of news and event analyses, publish the *Bulletin,* and produce a number of brochures and other written materials, as well. Although Benton's overarching Public and Cultural Relations concentrated on providing publications, teachers, libraries, and broadcasts for audiences abroad, it also produced a program for U.S. citizens on NBC entitled *Our Foreign Policy* that featured State Department personnel. In turn, the Division of Publications in the Office of Public Affairs sent out press releases of the program's transcripts. Through the Division of Historical Research, the office published the *Foreign Relations* series that made historical documents, including those that had once been classified, available to the public. Finally, the Division of Public Liaison wrote responses to mail addressed to the State Department or to the White House on issues of foreign policy and provided points of contact between the department and the public. Once each year, Public Liaison invited two hundred U.S. opinion leaders, typically individuals who headed national organizations, to a conference where they would hear from State Department speakers. The division arranged for similar meetings on a smaller scale each week between individuals stationed in Washington, D.C., who represented national organizations, and State Department officials. At the same time, the Division for Public Liaison did its best to respond to requests for speakers from groups that represented the general public, such as the North Dakota Cattlemen's Association, for instance. Russell explained, "These were the days before television. You didn't get as a part of your daily fare the Government leaders the way you do now. It was something of an event for someone to come from Washington and talk about the reasons for various policies."[6]

Across all four divisions, the State Department in 1947 had an active public affairs program and, just as important, the Office of Public Affairs had support that came from the top. According to Russell, "Acheson was always 1,000 percent behind the public affairs program. He was generous in giving it his time, in accepting speech requests, and creating an atmosphere in the Department whereby all other officers knew they were expected to cooperate." Marshall, too, was "absolutely wonderful" in meeting with Russell and with outside groups, and Truman himself met with groups on occasion because he valued the program so much.[7]

The Role of Public Affairs at State in Formulating Policy on Greece

In the context of proposing aid to Greece and Turkey, Truman faced a largely hostile Congress and a public uninterested in foreign involvement. He, his advisors, and the State Department were naturally concerned, therefore, about winning over public opinion. The high-level support for the Office of Public Affairs, however, led to a remarkable turn of events: policy-operations officers and public information officers working together on the formation of policy. On Tuesday, February 25, Acheson held a meeting at State to get "key political, economic, legal, and information officers" involved in the process of developing a more specific set of recommendations for the president. Russell, director of the Office of Public Affairs, and Joseph Jones, also of Public Affairs, were in attendance. At that meeting and others, information officers from the Office of Near Eastern and African Affairs and the Office of European Affairs participated, along with policy and operations officers, in the formation of policy and strategy. Although State had given new prominence to Public Affairs in recent years, the fact that individuals from all these groups collaborated on the Greek-Turkish issue was extraordinary because "a seldom-bridged chasm, wide and deep, between policy-operations work and information activity" still existed in the day-to-day workings of the State Department, where Public Affairs officers may have been considered mere flacks whose task was to sell the policy that others had formulated.[8] In the development of both the Truman Doctrine policy and the campaign to win its support, however, Public Affairs would prove to be a key player.

Acheson also wielded an immense amount of influence among the State Department officers working on the issue. In addition to serving as under secretary of state and also acting secretary of state during the frequent absences of Byrnes and later Marshall, Acheson had been an attorney, under secretary of the treasury, assistant secretary of state for Economic Affairs, and assistant secretary of state to maintain congressional relations and to oversee diplomatic conferences. He had been highly successful in all of these endeavors, which had earned him "an enviable and deserved reputation" in the Department.[9]

As Acheson overviewed the situation in Greece and Turkey during the meeting of February 25, he also demonstrated his rhetorical skill in getting all of the officers and staff on the same page. The under secretary of state described the problem and "alternate courses of action" by which the United States might respond. According to Jones, Acheson encouraged everyone to state his opinions, ask questions, and provide criticism of the possible policies. Jones recalled, "When all had spoken, Acheson made his summation, in the process allaying doubts, resolving conflicts, incorporating ideas presented to him, pointing up the logic of the discussion. Thus Acheson broadened his own conception of the problem and fortified his staff for creative work on the project ahead." Although Acheson already had his mind set on aiding Greece and Turkey, the under secretary's performance gave the appearance of open-mindedness; his encouragement of criticism also helped Acheson and the others consider more thoughtfully the best way to articulate the policy and to campaign for its adoption in order to achieve success. Acheson's compelling summation, furthermore, convinced the State Department staff members—many of whom were already predisposed to help Greece, including a few who had worked on the second memorandum given to Marshall and Truman the day before—that the course of action that Acheson supported was the best one. Jones described the impact: "Chief and staff were as one. There was only one point of view, and that was growing, evolving, from a free flow of ideas."[10] While Jones judged the meeting that afternoon as open and freewheeling, it appears instead, from the perspective of time, to have forged a committed consensus behind a policy path already chosen.

The State Department staff worked late to finalize a more detailed analysis of the Greek-Turkish situation and a set of recommendations to address it. According to the "Positions and Recommendations" report attached to the second memorandum, State believed there was only one choice, for if the United States did not step in, there would be "a widespread collapse of resistance to Soviet pressure throughout the Near and Middle East and large parts of western Europe" and possibly a British accommodation with the Soviets. Marshall approved the report and discussed it with Patterson and Forrestal on Wednesday, February 26. In turn, the secretaries of state, war, and the navy wrote a memorandum to the president that repeated, in more concise form, the steps contained in State's "Position and Recommendations" report. The secretaries recommended that the United States talk to the British about the situation and their intentions; determine how much the British could continue to help Greece and Turkey; inform the cabinet, especially the secretaries of treasury and commerce, of the situation and seek their input; find ways to help Greece financially and with military supplies and equipment that did not require legislation; ensure that the Greek government formally request the economic assistance of the United States (the secretaries did not mention the need for Turkey to do so); discuss the problem "privately and frankly" with "appropriate members of Congress"; draft legislation, on the basis of the discussion with congressional leaders and the input of the combined chiefs of staff; and, finally, adopt measures "to acquaint the American public with the situation and with the need for action along the proposed lines," presumably the statements made in the "Positions and Recommendations" report. The chiefs of staff had approved the course of action, as well. After discussing all of this with Acheson and Marshall, Truman agreed to the plan. Dwight Eisenhower, the army chief of staff, had suggested that the administration ask for funds to help other countries, as well, but the president and his men feared that the prospect of gaining aid for Greece and Turkey would be difficult enough given the time constraints posed by Greece's critical condition. They did recommend, however, that the idea be given further study. In the meantime, Truman asked that the relevant steps for extending aid to Greece and Turkey be put into action.[11]

First Congressional Meeting: February 27, 1947

The next day, at 10:00 A.M., the president, Marshall, and Acheson met with a select group of congressional leaders that included Senators Tom Connally, Styles Bridges, and Arthur Vandenberg; Speaker Joseph Martin; and Congressmen Charles Eaton, Sol Bloom, and Sam Rayburn. Conspicuously missing from the group was Sen. Robert Taft, who had not been invited. According to Acheson, Taft's absence was "accidental," an oversight on the part of the administration, but a more likely explanation is that he was not invited because he was apt to express his vociferous opposition to the proposed new policy and, as a leading presidential contender for 1948, had a great deal of clout in the Republican Senate. Vandenberg pointed out the omission and suggested that Taft be part of any future conferences.[12]

What happened next in the course of the meeting has been a subject for speculation ever since. According to Acheson, Secretary of State Marshall "most unusually and unhappily, flubbed his opening statement," leaving the congressional leaders unimpressed with the problem that the United States faced in Greece and Turkey. The under secretary saw the need to convince the men as crucial. As he later recalled, "I knew we were met at Armageddon. . . . In desperation I whispered to him [Marshall] a request to speak. This was my crisis. For a week I had nurtured it. These congressmen had no conception of what challenged them; it was my task to bring it home." Perhaps only Richard Nixon would dramatize and personalize crisis more. Acheson's memoirs restated his arguments, which relied on conceptions of violation, illness, and infection. He warned about the dangers of a Soviet "breakthrough" and "penetration" and compared the possible "corruption" of Greece to the way that "apples in a barrel infected by one rotten one" would "carry the infection" to the others. After he finished speaking, the leaders understood, Acheson said, and recommended that Truman make the case both to Congress and citizens. Jones provided a similar scenario of the meeting, for Acheson quickly regaled the State Department staff under him with the tale of how he had intervened. In his presentation at State, Acheson emphasized the threat posed by Soviet "possibilities for penetration," how the Soviets could "pull the plug" on France at any time, and the potential for a "complete collapse" of Greece. He also compared the current situation to the conflict between Carthage and Rome, with a similar impact on his listeners.[13]

The versions of the meeting recounted both directly by Acheson and indirectly through Jones are intriguing, because their portrayal of a dramatic personal intervention on the part of the under secretary does not comport with other accounts of the meeting. Both Truman and Vandenberg record that Marshall was the one who presented the case for Greece and Turkey, and they make no mention of Acheson speaking. Likewise, on March 12, Lyle Wilson of the *Washington Daily News* would trace the evolution of the crisis and report that it was Marshall at the congressional meeting who "sounded the alarm." Even more intriguing, Jones credited Acheson as concluding his presentation with

"The choice is between acting with energy or losing by default," but both Truman and Vandenberg attributed this statement to Marshall, and a copy of Marshall's presentation, which he submitted to Truman on February 27, includes that line.[14]

What should one make of this disparity? After all, Marshall's statement certainly encouraged listeners to understand that Greece was a crisis. At the very start, the secretary said, "A crisis of the utmost importance and urgency has arisen in Greece and to some extent in Turkey. This crisis has a direct and immediate relation to the security of the United States." Marshall also made use of some of the metaphors that Acheson employed when he referred to the imminent "collapse" of Greece and the threat to its "integrity." At the same time, Marshall's statement was not nearly as emotional as the arguments that Acheson claimed to use and was more bureaucratic in tone. He cautioned the congressional leaders, "If Greece should dissolve into civil war it is altogether probable that it would emerge as a communist state under Soviet control. Turkey would be surrounded and the Turkish situation, to which I shall refer in a moment, would in turn become still more critical." While Marshall clearly was discussing the domino theory here, his words lacked the drama of Acheson's warnings about rotten apples and Communist infection spreading throughout the world. The secretary's statement may well have been written by Henderson, who had been the primary drafter of memoranda on Greece for the past week. Recall, too, that Acheson found the need to change the title of Henderson's original memo—completed before the arrival of the British notes—and to edit the document in order to make it more compelling. Moreover, Marshall's matter-of-fact delivery of the statement may have seemed, as Acheson later described it, "rather crisp" and "rather cold" to his under secretary. One of the few exceptions to Marshall's more bureaucratic style in his February 26 statement was the line that Acheson attributed to himself—"The choice is between acting with energy or losing by default"—language that does sound very much like Acheson and, in fact, may have been suggested by him.[15] In the days that followed, Acheson would become increasingly involved in crafting administration arguments on behalf of Greek-Turkish aid for reporters and for the public message that Truman intended to give. Acheson also was, by many accounts, not a modest man. Although he probably did speak in the meeting with congressional leaders, it seems unlikely that he played as big a role as he suggested later that week to his State Department staff or years later in his memoirs.

Nonetheless, the versions of the meeting recalled by Acheson and Jones are interesting because they demonstrate the degree to which metaphors of disease and violation became lenses through which to view the issue of Greece. These linguistic framing devices are present in the memoranda drafted by Henderson and in Marshall's statement but appear far more often in the scenario described by Acheson to Jones and other staffers shortly after and yet more frequently still in Acheson's memoir intended to reveal the actual behind-the-scenes events that influenced public policy.[16] This evolution is also symptomatic of Acheson's impact on the administration's public messages about Greece. While Acheson's role at the White House meeting was far less than he claimed, it is possible that he *believed* his words had an impact on congressional leaders. Regardless, in his meeting with State Department staff on February 28, Acheson may have seen the effect that his retelling of the tale had on his listeners. Jones, who clearly admired Acheson, called it a "masterful" performance that outlined the themes that should be followed for the information program and presidential speech, but even Russell felt compelled to summarize Acheson's reenactment of the meeting with staffers as they began work later in the day. According to Jones, Acheson learned in his meeting with congressional leaders that "he had to pull out all the stops and speak in the frankest, boldest, widest terms to attract their support."[17] This lesson may have been learned or reinforced in Acheson's retelling of the tale to State Department personnel. In either event, the lesson had an impact on how State decided to present aid to Greece and Turkey to the public.

Another topic for speculation arising out of the meeting with congressional leaders is the question of what Vandenberg actually said to the president at the conference's conclusion. According to the senator, he and the other leaders made "general comments but no commitments," while Truman simply recalled that no one at the meeting disagreed with him when he said what he wanted to do. Acheson later claimed that Vandenberg told the president that if he were to repeat Acheson's arguments "to the Congress and the country, I will support you and I believe that most of its members will do the same." In the years to come, a popular story circulated that Vandenberg really told Truman there was only one way to get what he wanted and that was "to make a personal appearance before Congress and scare hell out of the country." Eric Goldman attributed this quotation to Vandenberg in his book, *The Crucial Decade,* but no other sources confirm that the senator ever really said it. The most accurate insight into the matter might come from messages that Acheson sent to Patterson and Marshall the week after the meeting. According to Acheson, the leaders "approve in principle the general program for aid" but wanted to meet with the president again once the administration had further details about its specific proposal.[18]

Although Press Secretary Ross had no official comment on the congressional meeting, Marshall spoke off the record afterwards with twenty reporters who regularly covered the State Department. He told them about the British note on Greece, the strategic importance of Greece, the decision to ask for aid, and the conference with congressional leaders. The next day, the Washington, D.C., papers reported that the meeting had taken place and speculated that a significant foreign policy decision was imminent. Vandenberg was quoted as saying only that "we had general discussion of European problems involved in approaching [the] Moscow meeting." James Reston of the *New York Times* reported many of the details of the request for aid to Greece in a front-page story the next day but provided no attribution, instead relying on phrases such as "it was learned tonight" and "it is understood." His words, too, though, seemed to reflect the dryer style of Marshall, for he wrote that "the failure by the United States to assume this economic burden might jeopardize the efforts of the last year to re-establish a balance of power with the Soviet Union in Europe."[19]

The New Policy and the Persuasive Campaign to Win Its Support

On Friday, February 28, the day the story broke, Acheson turned the State Department's attention to "preparing a concrete program of operation and explaining it to the Congress and the country." State Department staffers from the Offices of Near East and African Affairs, European Affairs, Economic Affairs, Public Affairs, Assistant Secretary of State for Occupied Areas, the Legal Division, and the Central Secretariat met together that morning. After Acheson's rousing account of the meeting with congressional leaders and analysis of the issues involved, he left, and Henderson and Hickerson made specific assignments. Russell was put in charge of the public information campaign. At the end of the meeting, Hickerson reminded everyone of the seriousness of the task before them, saying that Greece "was certainly the most important thing that had happened since Pearl Harbor." Jones recalled, "We all felt bowled over by the gravity of the situation and the immensity of all the steps that were contemplated."[20]

Afterwards, Russell immediately called a meeting of the Subcommittee on Foreign Policy Information of SWNCC (State-War-Navy Coordinating Committee), which he chaired. Other members included the information officers of the War and Navy Departments, but policy-operations officers from all three departments also were in attendance, as was Jones. At this point, the subcommittee did not concern itself with writing a presidential message but instead with the overall program of persuasion. According to Jones, "The specific tasks of the subcommittee were to draw together background information from the three Departments relating to all aspects of the program, to point out the main obstacles to public acceptance and suggest how to overcome them, to define the program of aid contemplated, to draft the themes to be used in the public approach, to consider what the lines of Soviet propaganda would be and how to counter them, and to prepare information programs for getting the story over to the press, radio, periodicals, and group leaders throughout the country." Furthermore, the subcommittee believed that what President Truman said and what "supporting speeches and documents before Congress and in institutional information programs" said should be consistent and mutually reinforce one another. After a great deal of discussion, Russell drafted a section on the policy proposed, Llewellyn Thompson of European Affairs wrote a description of the current situation in Greece, and Henry Villard of Near East and African Affairs put together a background of Greece's problems. John Jernegan of the Office of European Affairs also had a hand in the final version. Unfortunately, only a copy of Russell's section has survived, but it reveals just how much impact the director of public affairs had, not only on how the president's new foreign policy was depicted to the public but on the policy itself.[21]

Acheson had asked Russell to consider "how to couch the existing world conflict," but he also had recommended that it be described in broader terms as a question of protecting democracy and "our whole way of life."[22] When SWNCC's Subcommittee on Foreign Policy Information finished its report, entitled "Informational Objectives and Main Themes," Russell's section on "Basic United States Policy" appeared to follow Acheson's advice. It laid out a number of premises that appeared in future messages, and, as we will see later, Truman's address to Congress would even borrow much of Russell's wording.

In his section of the report, the director for public affairs listed fifteen themes to be used in the explanation of administration policy. He wrote, for example, "A cardinal objective of United States foreign policy is a world in which nations shall be able to work out their own way of life free of coercion by other nations." While this was an idea that Truman had voiced in his Navy Day address of 1945, it took on new meaning in light of the situation that Russell described. He depicted a frightening, polarized world in which there was "a conflict between two ways of life," one of which was based upon "the will of the majority" and freedom and the other on the "imposition of the will of a minority upon the majority" and oppression. As a result, Russell stated that it was the policy of the United States to help besieged people in their "struggle for freedom," whether the threat they faced was "fascist, nazi, communist, or of any other form." His informational guidelines, in fact, equated the policy of extending aid to Greece with Allied efforts against the Axis powers in World War II in an attempt to project its consistency with foreign policy from the past and insisted it was essential if the United States were to "maintain its freedom and security." Russell also argued that U.S. policy was consistent with the U.N. Charter and the United Nations' efforts at reconstruction. According to the thirteenth informational guideline, "The United States will continue to support and work through the United Nations in every way possible." The discussions in the working groups at State and, especially, in the SWNCC Subcommittee on Foreign Policy Information, had likely recognized that a possible criticism of the new policy would be that the United States should go through the United Nations rather than acting unilaterally. Russell's informational guidelines attempted to combat such an argument. Finally, the document suggested a theme intended to reassure listeners that the new policy did not mean war was imminent. Russell wrote, "A policy based upon the interdependence of free peoples does not necessarily betoken an increase in world tension nor an approach to war." Rather, "free countries of the world, whether free enterprise or not, can co-exist peacefully provided there is no plan of conquest, domination or infiltration by any of them. The United States desires earnestly to effect with the Soviet Union a thorough going understanding that will promote such a peaceful living together. It hopes and believes this can be done."[23] While reassuring, this line of argument suggested that the Soviet Union was a democracy, a statement that would have been news to individuals living under Stalin and unlikely to be accepted by American citizens who had emigrated, say, from Poland or Rumania. This shortcoming notwithstanding, Russell's expression of U.S. policy—informed by others on the SWNCC subcommittee—was compelling in its simplicity and in its appeals to freedom, compassion, and fear. It elevated the proposal of extending aid to Greece to a much broader plain, as Acheson had suggested. On this plain, the ambiguities of Greece's political situation were replaced with a commitment to unambiguous principle. The director of public affairs had, in effect, defined U.S. policy.

On March 3, the SWNCC subcommittee submitted its proposed public information campaign to Acheson who, in turn, approved it. The details of how the subcommittee intended to convey its informational themes to the public are not known, but they clearly included having the president speak, for Jones and others had begun writing drafts on Sunday, March 2. Furthermore, the plan relied on stimulating favorable news coverage through background briefings of the press. Acheson regularly began meeting with small groups of reporters, newspaper columnists, and radio commentators on February 27 and continued to do so in the weeks leading up to Truman's address.[24]

News Coverage Advances the Administration's Cause

Judging from media coverage, Acheson used the themes that Russell had developed, further enhanced by his own alarmist language, to create the desired impression. First, journalists depicted the situation as "the gravest crisis." Greece seemed all the more urgent since it had come as a "surprise," "suddenly," "like a bolt from the blue," and "a slap in the face." In addition, news coverage warned of Soviet expansionism and discussed the issue involved as one of Communism versus freedom. ABC's Earl Godwin, for instance, commented that the Truman administration was working toward peace but "everywhere the Russians stand right in the road," and numerous print and radio pieces invoked the domino theory. Columnist Ernest Lindle warned of a "chain reaction" that could "reach into Italy, France—into all of Europe and into other areas where Communism has a foothold," while commentator Gabriel Heatter warned that if Greece fell, the "world we believe in and fought to save will be gone."[25]

Some coverage depicted the situation in especially dramatic, frightening ways that relied upon the linguistic frameworks that Acheson had used. In a cover story, *Newsweek* described how the State Department was working "desperately to convince Congress and the American people that the germ disease of another world war had already taken root—this time in Greece." Hanson Baldwin of the *New York Times* warned in what purported to be a news story, rather than an editorial, that Germany was a "slowly starving cancerous growth in western Europe," still recovering from fascism and festering with "the virus of communism." While the Soviets were currently weaker than the United States, he contended, the situation could change if "the heart and soul and spirit and will of the American people succumb to decay."[26] When the media reported, without attribution, on March 2 that the State Department had agreed in principle to aid Greece, coverage depicted this policy as necessary for U.S. security. Radio commentator H. R. Baikhage said the United States must assume "the white man's burden" that Britain was abandoning or run "a very good chance of submitting to a Communist peace." Similarly, an editorial in the *New York Times* opined, "We are dealing with a civilization which might collapse. We are menaced by chaos. For our own self-preservation, if for no nobler motive, we have to be generous and courageous."[27]

While news coverage of Greece overwhelmingly followed these lines, occasional alternative perspectives also circulated. For example, a report—filed in Athens by Constantine Poulos and published by *New Republic*—argued that the blame for Greece's problems were primarily the fault of its own government. According to Poulos, "Profits on private imports, which are financed by government funds, run from 200 to 800 percent. With these enormous profits, importers, industrialists and brokers buy and hoard gold sovereigns from the government, further depleting the monetary reserve." Moreover, Poulos reported that the "Royalist right-wing government," as soon as it became convinced that the United States was backing it, "arrested, sentenced and deported to island prisons nearly 600 leftists." He argued that the Greek government, rather than Soviet scheming, was responsible for civil unrest. As Poulos observed, "Two bitterly full years of the exploitation of men who fought the Germans by men who collaborated with Germans have driven more Greeks into the mountains than all the encouragement from the 'north.'"[28]

Exceptions like this aside, however, news coverage in the two weeks prior to Truman's March 12 speech largely reflected the views perpetuated by the White House for a number of reasons. First, administration officials were now united in their perspectives on Greece, which meant that reporters could not play the views of a Forrestal against those of a Wallace. The inclusion of the internationally minded Vandenberg and the exclusion of the isolationist and influential Taft at the first meeting with congressional leaders also made it more difficult for opposition views to be voiced in a meaningful way.

Second, the administration's use of background briefings before it made any formal announcement of policy encouraged coverage that supported its point of view. In lieu of largely absent alternative interpretations, the briefings shaped the way in which journalists covered Greece, while the background nature of the administration's communication meant that critics of a new policy had no official statements toward which they could clearly direct a public response. Some members of Congress, like Rep. Albert Engel of Michigan, vocally opposed "pulling Britain's 'fat out of the fire' in Greece." More typical, however, were the responses like that of Senator Taft who merely stated that aid to Greece "would involve a tremendous change in policy and I would not like to say now how I stand on it until I have all of the facts." Reporter Bertram Hulen noted, "For the moment, the attitude in Congress is one of reserve but deep concern and anxiety."[29] After the first congressional meeting and background briefings to the press, five days elapsed before the administration commented officially; Truman would not meet with congressional leaders again for six days after that. Moreover, two additional days would pass between the second meeting with the congressional leadership and the president's address to Congress and the nation as a whole. The timing of the media briefings heightened the administration's rhetorical advantage by not providing specifics on proposed aid that opponents could critique as, simultaneously, the briefings perpetuated the atmosphere of crisis and shaped coverage of Greece in a way that supported the White House point of view.

A third factor contributing to favorable coverage was how journalists had come to see their professional roles. During World War II, many journalists worked for the Office of War Information (OWI), the U.S. wartime propaganda agency that dealt primarily with international audiences but also targeted domestic audiences, too. With the close of the war and the OWI, these individuals returned to their work in the news media but with far more positive views about the role of government-media cooperation in pursuit of the national interest. Likewise, at the *New York Times*, editors and owners permitted incredibly skewed coverage of Greece because they believed it was important to convince the public of the seriousness of protecting U.S. national security.[30]

Yet another variable was that a number of reporters had personal relationships with government officials that, in turn, shaped their views. James Reston of the *New York Times* is a case in point. As political scientist Daniel Chomsky pointed out, Reston's memoirs proudly pointed to his easy access to government officials—how the journalist regularly ran into Acheson on his morning walks and frequently stopped to visit with Vandenberg, who lived near Reston, for example. Chomsky noted, "Reston repeatedly suggested that he used his prominent friends as sources; he seemed unaware that they may have used him." Indeed, Reston's stories largely reflected the administration's perspective at the very start and, once Vandenberg was on board, what Jones referred to as Reston's "close relationship with Senator Vandenberg" would prove most useful to the White House.[31]

Finally, as noted earlier, U.S. history provided a rich rhetorical stockpile of anti-Communist imagery and language, as well as the polarizing rhetoric used only recently to attack fascism, on which opinion leaders—including journalists—could readily draw. Truman's refusal to address U.S.-Soviet relations had left a vacuum that his political opponents had readily filled to his detriment. Now that the president had decided to act, however, the linguistic and conceptual frameworks provided by this rhetorical stockpile worked to his advantage by supporting the administration's change in policy.

All in all, then, a number of variables influenced radio and press coverage in the weeks prior to Truman's speech, leading to coverage that promoted the administration's point of view. As Jones later reflected, the news coverage "encouraged those engaged in articulating and implementing the policy and performed an invaluable service as advance agent to Congress and the public for the President's message of March 12."[32] At the same time, media stories worked to the disadvantage of liberals and anti-Communist, isolationist Republicans who opposed the administration.

Marshall Officially Goes Public with the Crisis

As plans for offering aid to Greece commenced behind the scenes, Secretary of State Marshall prepared to leave for the Council of Foreign Ministers conference in Moscow. He made use of his press statement prior to his departure, however, to go public officially about matters that had, until that point, been shared with reporters on background only. As Marshall stood at the door of his airplane on March 4, he announced, "the economic condition of Greece has deteriorated to the verge of collapse. In light of the world situation, this is a matter of primary importance to the United States." The secretary of state noted that Truman and the executive branch were giving the matter their "urgent attention" and had discussed it with "appropriate Congressional leaders." Marshall's words gave credence to the press reports that Greece constituted a crisis, depicting it as a crucial issue to the United States and to the administration, which was capably working to resolve the matter in cooperation with the legislative branch. In closing, the secretary of state prepared listeners for Truman's upcoming message and clearly conveyed that the president was in charge. According to Marshall, "I cannot say anything today regarding the action which may be taken, other than that a full public statement will be made very soon, when the executive agencies have completed their consideration of the matter. The problems involved are so far-reaching and of such transcendent importance that any announcement relating to them could properly come only from the President himself." Still, Marshall did not want to give the impression that the Truman administration was doing an end run around Congress, whose support it needed. He ended his statement, "The final decisions will rest with the President and the Congress." After his departure, the State Department publicly released the message from Greece that requested U.S. assistance, an appeal that the State Department had itself drafted and then asked the Greek government to submit, to underscore further the media and administration messages of the preceding days.[33]

In news coverage of Marshall's statement, reporters depicted the secretary as "determined," "grim and thoughtful" as he stressed the "vital" need to extend aid to Greece. Press accounts perpetuated the aura of crisis as they struggled for analogies. In *New Republic*, readers learned that "the events attending Secretary Marshall's departure for Moscow sobered and frightened Washington more deeply than anything since the fall of France," while *Newsweek* alluded to the Manchurian crisis of 1931 and the U.S. failure to stop early Japanese expansion in Asia, declaring "The United States this week stood on the threshold of a policy decision on which the future peace of the world would unquestionably hang." In *Life*, the coverage portrayed Marshall as having the air of "a man who bears a heavy burden. . . . The U.S. had suddenly come up against a diplomatic crisis, requiring momentous decisions all around the world." Once again the administration, aided by the news media, had succeeded in conveying the message that Greece constituted an urgent issue of overarching significance that the administration could not have reasonably anticipated. And though Marshall's public statement had emphasized the economic troubles of Greece, General Eisenhower met with newspaper reporters later that day and outlined, on a background basis, the military importance of that country, as well. Shortly thereafter, articles began discussing the strategic significance of Greece to protecting Turkey and of Turkey to accessing the Dardanelles and the Mediterranean and its oil supplies. The term "containment" also started to appear in some news coverage to describe the administration's apparent policy.[34] Eisenhower's briefing, along with those that Acheson continued to hold, undoubtedly served to heighten further the implications of Greece in the eyes of journalists.

Truman's Illness in the Midst of Crisis

On the day that Marshall went public with the crisis, the president was out of town. Truman had left on March 2 in the middle of a major snowstorm in Washington, D.C.—despite feeling poorly from the aftermath of an upper respiratory infection—for Grandview, Missouri, to visit his mother who had recently broken her hip. The next day, he proceeded on a successful trip to Mexico as the first U.S. president ever to visit that country. On March 6, Truman arrived in Waco, Texas, from Mexico City in weather that *Newsweek* described as "cold, wet, and nasty," which did little to improve how he felt. In a diary discovered decades later and released in 2003, the president's entry for that day reveals that his physician, Dr. Wallace Graham, had just informed Truman that he had a more permanent condition. The president wrote, "Doc tell's [sic] me I have Cardiac Asthma! Ain[']t that hell. Well it makes no diff[erence,] will go on as before. I've sworn him to secrecy! So What!"[35]

The reason for the secrecy may have been that cardiac asthma is, in actuality, not asthma at all but breathing difficulty deriving from weakness in the heart's left ventricle, which can then result in pulmonary edema or fluid in the lungs and symptoms such as "difficult wheezing respiration, pallor, and anxiety." According to Dr. George Sopko, a cardiologist at the National Institutes of Health, physicians during Truman's time would have treated such a condition with diuretics to dry out his lungs—or with digoxin to help the left ventricle perform better—and with rest. As noted earlier, Dr. Graham, the president's personal physician, had occasionally given Truman diuretics to eliminate fluid in his lungs; he said he stayed with the president all night long as Truman sat up and coughed. Eben Ayers also recorded a chance meeting with the president at Graham's White House office in the spring of 1947, where Truman explained that he occasionally sought chest diathermy treatment, in which an electric current was used to create heat in the tissues below the skin, to treat "a congested condition in his chest which is causing him some trouble and which has from time to time caused some annoyance." According to Graham, Truman was healthy, aside from these periodic difficulties with his lungs—Graham never mentioned cardiac asthma in his 1989 oral history interview—but the physician did admit that he intentionally withheld information about his treatment of Truman's congestion problems from the press.[36]

Truman, of course, lived another twenty-five years, which raises the question of whether he really had anything substantially wrong with his heart. His longevity, vigorous walks, and typical image of outward fitness seem to belie any claims of serious long-term illness, despite his periodic bouts with lung congestion. According to Kenneth Shafer, MD, a cardiologist at Cleveland Clinic, heart disease was difficult to diagnose at the time. In fact, Margaret Truman reported that navy doctors concluded her father had a heart ailment in 1937, but that army doctors subsequently disagreed. Graham, too, reported that a navy physician had warned him when he took over Truman's care in 1945 that "the man you're to take care of will not live through the Presidency" because Truman "had pulmonary edema" or fluid trapped in his lungs due to a malfunctioning heart. Shafer explains that a great deal of confusion over diagnosis often existed and, in retrospect, it is hard to know the cause of Truman's problems. If Dr. Graham thought the president's lungs were not at fault, he may have placed the blame on Truman's heart. Conversely, if tests had definitively shown that Truman had congestive heart problems in 1947, Shafer says it is highly unlikely that the president would have lived another quarter of a century.[37]

One possibility, however, is that Truman had a "reaction to a viral infection, causing a transient decrease in heart function." Individuals who respond to viruses in this way may find the effect on their hearts lasts several months or several years or is even permanent. According to Shafer, patients who suffer from post-viral cardiomyopathy tend to be more susceptible to other viruses and, even if their decrease in heart function is temporary, their hearts may respond similarly to subsequent viruses. This tendency could explain why army doctors gave Truman a clean bill of health, while navy doctors—examining him on a different occasion—concluded he had heart problems. Similarly, Graham recounted that Truman suffered lung congestion only occasionally, particularly early in his presidency, rather than constantly. Consistent with the characteristics of post-viral cardiomyopathy, the president also was highly susceptible to viruses. In December 1947, the *New York Times* commented that correspondents considered Truman to be "in robust health" but with a "tendency to coughs and colds." The newspaper reported that White House officials had just placed two "ultra-violet-ray floor lamps" in Truman's office for that reason, reducing "the count of cold and influenza germs there by 62 per cent." According to Shafer, individuals with post-viral cardiomyopathy are vulnerable to stress, as well, which can then aggravate the problems of decreased heart function.[38] The Oval Office always puts ample pressure on its occupants, but Truman undoubtedly faced a particularly trying time given the challenges of 1945–47 and his own predisposition to suffer from stress. While any attempt to diagnose Truman's health problems after the fact are speculative, of course, the possibility of post-viral cardiomyopathy is certainly consistent with the symptoms that the president appeared to exhibit and what is publicly known about his health history.

In March 1947, the president and his physician were especially sensitive to public perceptions of Truman's health for several reasons. First, Franklin Roosevelt had died in office less than two years prior, after a period of decline, which no doubt made the public and the White House more attentive to perceptions of Truman's well-being. This may have been especially so since Truman was nearly sixty-two when he assumed the presidency, only a year younger than FDR at his death and the oldest entering president since Benjamin Harrison in 1857. In addition, Truman had no vice president during his first term in office, a fact that likely weighed on his mind considerably. The president seemed aware of just how important it was that he stay well, telling White House usher J. B. West, "A man in my position has a public duty to keep himself in good condition."[39]

Given Truman's illness at the time, one cannot help but wonder if the state of the president's health, in some small way, did not also serve to reinforce his decision to aid Greece and Turkey. The president recognized that outward appearances could be deceiving, for he attempted to convey an image of vitality in February and March of 1947, yet he knew—whatever the reason—that he was not well. Just as Truman's health and illness battled for supremacy, he had come to perceive a struggle between freedom and Communism in Greece and elsewhere that belied most American citizens' perceptions that democracy was robust and that the Soviet Union posed no threat.

Truman's diary entry in Waco and the diagnosis of cardiac asthma make clear that Graham was concerned with fluid buildup in the president's lungs, regardless of its cause, in March 1947. The fact that the president did not feel well may have been apparent to journalists covering him, as well, for the administration appeared to overcompensate with positive public comments about his health. On March 3 in Mexico City, Dr. Graham appeared with Charlie Ross before reporters and announced, according to the *New York Times,* that "from the standpoint of health, the President was like a man twenty years younger than his actual age of 63," a statement that strained credulity.[40] Ironically, the Truman administration sought to downplay any perceptions of his personal illness at the same time that it had begun a campaign to convince Congress, the press, and the public that Greece was on the verge of collapse.

Regardless of how he felt, Truman went forward with his itinerary in Waco, delivering what Ayers said was intended to be "an important, major" speech on free enterprise at Baylor University. The president did not mention Greece in his address, but he sounded several themes compatible with the administration's ongoing work on the crisis. According to Truman, the time for both political and economic isolationism had ended. He argued for the establishment of the International Trade Organization (ITO), under U.N. auspices, to prevent economic warfare among nations and to foster free enterprise. As "the giant of the economic world," the United States needed to provide bipartisan support for international economic cooperation. Truman explained, "Our foreign relations, political and economic, are indivisible. We cannot say that we are willing to cooperate in one field and unwilling to cooperate in the other. I am glad to note that the leaders in both parties have recognized that fact."[41] While Truman's goal at Baylor was to reinforce the need for bipartisan support of the ITO and to reassure Americans of the ITO's compatibility with free enterprise, his address also made clear that the United States could no longer isolate itself from the world and that politics and economics went hand in hand with foreign policy, premises on which the administration's upcoming proposal to offer aid to Greece would rest. Likewise, the president's call for bipartisanship was one borne of necessity in the case of both the ITO and Greece.

Truman's speech at Baylor was well received in the media. According to the State Department's Office of Public Affairs, initial press and radio reaction showed that it was "heartily acclaimed" for its emphasis on bipartisanship, American leadership, and free enterprise. The "round-up" of media responses included excerpts of favorable coverage from outlets such as the *Washington Post,* the *Baltimore Sun,* the *New York Times, St. Louis Star-Times, Richmond Times-Dispatch,* the *New York Herald Tribune,* the *Wall Street Journal, New Orleans Times-Picayune,* ABC, and CBS, among others. On ABC, Martin Agronsky made explicit the underlying parallels with a potential new policy on Greece. He said that Truman's speech had voiced a "new and revolutionary concept of a policy of intervention by America outside the Western Hemisphere. The president specifically confines this American intervention to the economic field. But implicit in his speech there is . . . the recognition that economic intervention has political consequences."[42]

Despite its reinforcing themes, though, Truman's address was largely overlooked. The Division of Press Intelligence, in the Office of Government Reports, recounted that while editorial responses were overwhelmingly positive, Truman's words received relatively little attention because the Supreme Court decision upholding contempt charges against John L. Lewis and the United Mine Workers was announced, unexpectedly, just as the president began to speak. Again, ABC's Agronsky articulated the problem well. He observed, "Even a heavyweight championship fight would have to fight for headline space against the Lewis story and the President's speech seems so far on the losing end, as far as public interest is concerned."[43] Given how long Lewis had been a thorn in Truman's side, however, it is doubtful the president minded being upstaged all that much by a decision that affirmed the administration's stance. Truman may have been ill and feeling poorly, but the outcome of the Lewis case likely gave him a lift.

The Crisis Atmosphere Intensifies

Upon his return, Truman met with Acheson, Clifford, Treasury Secretary Snyder, and Leahy and settled on the figure of $250 million in aid for Greece and another $150 million in aid for Turkey. He and Acheson met with the cabinet about the matter on the morning of March 7, the day after the president's homecoming. Truman informed the secretaries of his decision and said, "This is only the beginning. It means U.S. going into European politics." As he spoke, Truman also emphasized the role that persuasion would play in getting public and congressional support. He said Greece represented "the greatest selling job ever facing a President" and asked for his team's opinions. Immediately, different members of the cabinet, while stating agreement with the policy, pointed out rhetorical problems that it posed. Snyder warned that the administration had to be "prepared to answer charges that we are saving British interests." Similarly, Interior Secretary Julius Krug worried that the decision to help Greece fight Communism might appear to be in conflict with the administration's earlier decision to pull out of China. Acheson replied that although the fundamentals of the two cases were the same, the "incidences are different." The president concurred. Truman blamed Chiang Kai-shek for lacking the resolve to "fight it out" against the Communists and said extending aid to the Chinese government "would be pouring sand in a rat hole under [the] present situation."[44] The responses of Acheson and Truman to Krug are significant, for they make clear the administration had no intention of applying what would become known as the Truman Doctrine everywhere around the globe.

By the cabinet meeting's close, Truman and his men had decided that a two-pronged approach to persuasion was needed before a presidential speech. First, Snyder would meet with Commerce Secretary Averell Harriman, Navy Secretary James Forrestal, Labor Secretary Lew Schwellenbach, Agriculture Secretary Clinton Anderson, and assistant to the president, John Steelman, to set up a board to get the business community's support for aid to Greece. As Forrestal put it, "We must draft the top businessmen to sell the program. The Govt can't do it alone." The group also would work to inform "selected groups" of U.S. diplomats of the situation so that they could speak in an informed and, presumably, uniform way about the issue. Second, Truman said he would prepare a presentation for the congressional leadership for Monday. After the cabinet meeting, Press Secretary Ross informed reporters that the president's planned Caribbean vacation had been "indefinitely postponed" because of "developments," but he refused to elaborate on what those developments were.[45] The atmosphere of crisis intensified.

Truman's return to the White House also coincided with growing impatience among journalists about the continuous background briefings on Greece in the absence of a direct presidential message. While Ross was with Truman in Mexico and Waco, Assistant Press Secretary Ayers was left in Washington, D.C., where he complained, "I am badgered with queries about the president's coming action in the Greek situation as a result of the British request for aid from the U.S. in the occupation of Greece. Newspapermen have rumors of all kinds and ask daily—several times a day—as to when there will be a statement or a message from the President." Even Reston grumbled that officials had explained the military and economic situation of Greece and Turkey "so that the story could be told to the people, but so far the Government has not taken responsibility for going to the country with the broad question and asking for its support." The White House dashed journalists' expectations further when Truman failed to discuss Greece in his address at Baylor.[46]

Second Congressional Meeting: March 10, 1947

On Monday, March 10, the president met again with congressional leaders, but this time Senator Taft was invited, along with Sen. Alben Barkley, Senator Connally, Sen. Kenneth McKellar, Senator Vandenberg, Sen. Wallace White, Speaker Martin, Rep. Charles Halleck, Representative Eaton, Representative Bloom, Rep. John Taber, Representative Rayburn, Rep. Clarence Cannon, and Rep. John McCormack. Because of his wife's death, Barkley declined the invitation and sent Sen. Scott Lucas of Illinois in his place, while Taber took the place of Styles Bridges, who was out of town. McKellar also was absent but for very different reasons. His anger over Truman's nomination of David Lilienthal to head the Atomic Energy Commission had led him to reject the meeting.[47]

When Truman laid out the administration's proposal, he encountered what Acheson said was "a cool and silent reception," despite the assurances that Vandenberg had offered in the first meeting. The president later recalled, however, only that no one had opposed the plan.[48] Truman's message likely did prompt a frosty response from Republicans like Speaker Martin, for the Republican-dominated Eightieth Congress had been swept to power on issues like the desire to cut taxes and to retreat from foreign obligations. At the same time, the president also had friends in the room, from staunch Democratic supporters like Rayburn to the internationally minded Vandenberg from the other side of the aisle. The relative silence with which the proposal to aid Greece and Turkey was met may also have been, in good part, a reaction to the ominous nature of the situation that the president depicted, particularly coming so soon after the end of the war.

When the congressional leadership departed, Vandenberg told reporters that Truman had discussed the proposed aid package with "great candor." The senator then preempted the White House by announcing that the president "will come to Congress at noon Wednesday to a joint session of the House and Senate to discuss the whole situation." Afterwards, Press Secretary Ross confirmed the planned speech but clarified that Truman would not start speaking until 1:00 P.M. on Wednesday, March 12. Ross added that the president's message was not yet in final form, a statement that not only allowed him to forestall specific questions about the speech's content but also had the virtue of being true.[49] In any event, many of the themes and arguments that would appear in Truman's address had already circulated widely as a result of background briefings to the press and the congressional leadership.

Conclusion

Starting with the first meeting of the Special Committee to Study Assistance to Greece and Turkey on February 21, the State Department and the White House had worked to establish a persuasive context in which Truman's upcoming speech could be understood. The selective invitations to the first congressional meeting, the background briefings for reporters, Marshall's statement prior to his departure for

Moscow, the administration's effort to get business leaders on board, and even Truman's largely overshadowed speech at Baylor and abrupt cancellation of his vacation promoted a sense of crisis and encouraged opinion leaders to perceive the situation in ways compatible with the administration's evolving policy. Reflecting on the attempt to create a "public build-up for a major policy change," Jones reflected, "News and radio men collected and spread the pollen of information and speculation among congressmen, government officials, and the public."[50] The special pains taken to coordinate messages and to aim for consistency in their content further added to the effectiveness of the conditioning. Nonetheless, these early persuasive efforts were just part of the administration's campaign to win support for aid to Greece and Turkey, for the president's address to Congress was also key, and officials at both State and the White House played instrumental roles in the construction of what would become Truman's most famous speech.

———◆·●·◆———

CHAPTER 4

Opportunity through Threat

The Evolution and Crisis Promotion
of the Truman Doctrine Speech

In Chinese, the character for "crisis" has a double meaning: threat *and* opportunity. The crisis characteristics of the Truman Doctrine speech would derive not only from the administration's perception of threat but also from its need to make use of a strategic opportunity. As noted earlier, Truman had emphasized to his cabinet on March 7 that the extension of aid to Greece and Turkey demanded a "selling job." Still, Elsey worried to Clifford on that same day, after he read State's draft of what he called an "all-out" speech for the president, that the timing was not right for such a message, in part because there had been "no overt action in the immediate past by the USSR which serves as an adequate pretext" and because there was insufficient time to prepare the public.[1]

Elsey was not alone in his concerns over the speech's potential impact. Despite the administration's consensus on the Soviet threat, not everyone approved of the fear-arousing language and likely consequences they saw in early drafts. Kennan, for example, read one of State's attempts at a presidential message and vehemently objected. While he supported economic aid to Greece, Kennan opposed the speech because of "the sweeping nature of the commitments which it implied," but his protests fell on deaf ears. Marshall and his assistant, Charles Bohlen, likewise received a cable in Paris with a draft of the intended address and, in turn, expressed their concerns. According to Bohlen, "It seemed to General Marshall and to me that there was a little too much flamboyant anti-Communism in the speech." Washington replied, however, that the administration—including Truman—did not think Congress would approve the legislation without it.[2]

In the end, the Truman Doctrine speech would be successful in helping the administration achieve its goals for a number of reasons, two of which are relevant here. First, although Elsey was unaware of details of the State Department's advance work with congressional leaders and journalists, its news management efforts—as chapter 3 demonstrated—established a receptive context for the upcoming address.[3] In addition, Elsey and the countless others who worked on Truman's speech crafted a message in which the dangers appeared sufficiently urgent to necessitate congressional action and public support.

Indeed, so many people were involved to some degree in the writing of the president's address that controversy would swirl around the authorship of the Truman Doctrine speech for years to come. Press accounts at the time it was delivered gave credit to various individuals. According to *Time* magazine, Marshall had drafted "three quarters of the speech," while *Newsweek* claimed State Department experts had written it under the supervision of Loy Henderson. The *New York Tribune* reported that Marshall, Acheson, and Clifford were the chief authors. In his 1955 book, *The Fifteen Weeks: An Inside Account of the Genesis of the Marshall Plan,* Jones gave primary credit of authorship to Acheson, who drew upon contributions from others, and to himself, as the one who "held the pen and master draft until the White House took over for editing." According to Jones, "The State Department drafted the message. The White House pointed it up and styled it for presidential delivery." Acheson's memoirs conveyed much the same impression.[4]

Not surprisingly, these claims did not sit well with either Elsey or Clifford. In a 1970 interview, Elsey complained that Jones had written a book in which "he patted himself on the back for the great speech he had written, and for his fine style that he thought the White House staff messed up." Elsey then critiqued Jones's prose and pointed out the value of his rewriting of Jones's draft. In 1997, Elsey provided a gentler assessment, that Jones was a "swift and skillful writer," but maintained that the changes he and Clifford made were significant. Clifford, ever the diplomat, responded to a 1971 question about Acheson's description of the drafting process with, "I would have a different recollection about that." At the same time, throughout his entire explanation of the drafting process, Clifford never once mentioned Elsey, although he later would do so in his 1991 *Counsel to the President.*[5]

For his part, even President Truman claimed an important role in the evolution of the address. He wrote in his memoirs that the first State Department draft read like "an investment prospectus." According to the president, when he read a later version, one sentence stood out: "'I believe that it should be the policy of the United States. . . . ' I took my pencil, scratched out 'should' and wrote in 'must.' In several other places I did the same thing. I wanted no hedging in this speech." Both Clifford and Elsey have politely disagreed with Truman's recollection, and their position is borne out by the examination of speech drafts available at the Truman Library.[6]

The State Department Begins the Drafting Process

The Truman Doctrine speech, after its initial draft, underwent eight major revisions in all, with countless numbers of individuals involved along the way. In the Truman administration, Carlin observed that primary responsibility for speechwriting lay with close advisers who tended to have "backgrounds in law, economics, and political science (as opposed to rhetoric and literature)." Presidents today hire individuals to do nothing but write speeches, whereas Truman's usual speechwriters were advisers who had many other responsibilities, as well. According to Clifford, he typically met with the president when a speech was to be written and took notes on what Truman wanted in the message. He said he (and his staff) would work on the message and also ask the relevant policy department to come up with a draft.[7]

In the case of the Truman Doctrine address, however, it appears that the procedure was different since the idea for a speech originated with State, specifically in the report that Henderson oversaw, "Positions and Recommendations of the Department of State Regarding Immediate Aid to Greece and Turkey," and that Acheson approved on February 23. The report not only argued the administration should extend aid to the two countries but also that it should make efforts to convince key members of Congress and to "acquaint the American public with the situation and the need for action." This was the report that Marshall and then Truman approved that got the campaign rolling. After soliciting feedback from the cabinet and the combined chiefs of staff, the president gave the green light to the proposal's implementation on February 26.[8]

Initially, the State Department considered both a message directed to Congress and a radio fireside chat to address the public. Before these could be planned, however, Henderson and Hickerson realized that the policy itself needed to be articulated, as well as the chief themes that any messages should include. They charged Russell of Public Affairs with planning the public information campaign and, as noted previously, he oversaw both policy-operations officers and information officers of the Subcommittee on Foreign Policy Information of SWNCC (State-War-Navy Coordinating Committee) to produce the report entitled, "Informational Objectives and Main Themes." Within this report, Russell wrote the section called "Basic United States Policy." This document, more than any other, served to define the Truman Doctrine. Jones, who sat in on the group's early meetings, would ultimately be responsible for ensuring consistency between the messages of Truman and other administration officials as they spoke to Congress, the media, and the public.[9]

On Sunday, March 2, three State Department officials started drafting the presidential message aimed at Congress: Henderson, Jones, and Gordon Merriam, also from the Office of Near Eastern and African Affairs. After Henderson provided Acheson with all three drafts, Acheson called Jones and asked him to undertake the job. Although Jones wrote only five pages—an attempt "to arrive at a tone"—in comparison to Henderson's and Merriam's complete drafts, an examination of the three texts makes it is easy to understand why Acheson selected Jones. First, Jones used much the same language that Acheson had used when he told State Department officers on February 28 about the meeting with congressional leaders. Jones's draft included Acheson's comparison of U.S.-Soviet relations to the conflict between Athens and Sparta, and Rome and Carthage, for example. In sum, Jones's attempt mirrored Acheson's own perceptions and language preferences. Second, Jones's draft, reflecting his public affairs background, was clearly better suited for a speech. Henderson's message did not even mention Greece until midway through page 8, an approach that would have left listeners wondering what the point of the speech was, while Merriam's draft employed vocabulary ill-suited to such an address. Merriam's draft explained, for instance, that while the United States had worked hard to make the United Nations "the dominant influence, arbiter and safeguard in international life, a considerable and unavoidable interregnum of hard work and evolution is required before such a state of affairs can be attained."[10] One can hardly imagine any successful politician employing such a phrase, let alone the plain-spoken Harry Truman.

On the afternoon of Tuesday, March 4, Acheson held a drafting conference in his office that included Jones and Russell, Hickerson and Llewellyn Thompson from the Office of European Affairs, Hubert Havlik from Economic Affairs, John Howard from the Legal Division, Ernest Gross from the Office of Assistant Secretary of State for Occupied Areas, and John Gange from the Central Secretariat, along with several other State Department officials. Jones had already begun revising his draft and, during the session, Acheson went through a number of documents that he thought Jones could draw upon: Merriam's and Henderson's drafts, the official appeal of the Greek government for aid (an appeal that had been written by the State Department to begin with), and what Jones referred to as State's "Positions and Recommendations" memorandum, but which actually appears to have been Russell's "Basic United States Policy." From Merriam's draft, they pulled a roughly written paragraph describing the condition in which German troops left Greece when they retreated; this paragraph, with its mention of a starving, tubercular population and burned villages, came from a March 3 background memorandum on Greece. Jones's official March 4 draft, completed after the initial speech conference, would feature a more polished depiction, drawing upon both Merriam and the memo. An examination of Henderson's version reveals that Acheson and company chose the sentence, "It would be unutterably tragic for countries which have heroically struggled for their independence against overwhelming odds during the war years to lose after the victory that for which they had sacrificed so much," which was very similar to the line that eventually ended up in Truman's speech: "It would be an unspeakable tragedy if these countries, which have struggled so long against overwhelming odds, should lose that victory for which they sacrificed so much." As we will see, this was not the only offering from Henderson's draft that would find its way into the final version. From the appeal for aid from Greece, Acheson, Jones, and the others took the list of aid items that were being requested, a version of which appeared in Jones's March 4 draft.[11]

The most important of the documents on which the drafting conference drew, however, was Russell's "Basic United States Policy" from "Informational Objectives and Main Themes." According to Jones, Acheson lifted from the report, almost verbatim, what later became a major section of Truman's speech. A comparison of Russell's document with Jones's March 4 draft and the March 12 speech that Truman actually delivered confirms the impact that Russell had on both the Truman Doctrine and the president's address. In his prose, Russell enunciated the key principles of the Truman Doctrine. He stated that an important objective of U.S. foreign policy was a world where countries were free from coercion by others; he divided the world into two camps—the free who follow the will of the majority and the totalitarian minority that imposes its will on others; he argued that the Truman Doctrine was consistent with U.S. efforts in World War II and with the U.N. Charter; and, finally, Russell declared that it was the policy of the United States "to give support to free peoples who are attempting to resist subjugation from armed minorities or from outside forces" primarily through economic means. In his March 4 text, Jones had used the line on U.S. policy verbatim, but Jones and Acheson in their marked-up copies of the March 4 text changed "It is the policy of the United States" to "I believe that it must be the policy of the United States. . . ." This, of course, would eventually develop into the most famous section of the speech. Interestingly, though, it was Henderson who first used this phrasing. His draft of the speech stated, "I furthermore firmly believe that the United States must be prepared to give similar assistance to other democratic countries who may require our aid to preserve their independence, particularly when it is clear that the preservation of their independence is important to the interests of the United States."[12] Taken as a whole, however, Truman's address clearly drew most heavily upon Russell to articulate exactly what the Truman Doctrine was, the world conditions that called for it, and the ways in which the Truman Doctrine was consistent with U.S. interests and values.

How much involvement Russell, Henderson, and the others had in the remainder of the speechwriting process at State is not entirely clear. Although Jones's private accounts of his work indicate that Acheson told him to "keep in close touch with Henderson" as he wrote, Jones's book claimed that Acheson asked Jones "to undertake the task under his [Acheson's] direction." No archival evidence provides insight on any specific advice that State officials other than Acheson may have continued to give Jones, although Jones did write that his March 6 draft was approved by both Henderson and Hickerson before it went to Acheson.[13]

The second drafting conference, the one that changed "It is the policy" to "I believe it must be the policy," took place on the afternoon of Wednesday, March 5, in Acheson's office. Although some of the same individuals from the first drafting conference were present, Jones reported that it was a smaller group and that Acheson led them through "a line by line consideration of the draft." Acheson's annotated copy of the March 4 draft from this conference also indicates that the under secretary of state spent time writing passages in longhand that might be used. Not surprisingly, his contributions consisted largely of polarized appeals to heighten the significance of the decision to extend aid. Acheson wrote, for example, "There are countries in Europe whose peoples are struggling against *difficulties* & impediments & with patriotic courage to maintain their freedoms . . . while they repair the ravages of war. Should Greece fail in her struggle the effect may be far reaching to the West as well as to the East."[14] These lines and several others penned by Acheson during the drafting conference would survive, in edited form, in the final text.

After the March 5 session, Jones began preparing a third draft of the speech but was uncertain as to how he should word the sentences that asked for financial assistance. He did not know if the address should ask for a specific number of dollars for just Greece *or* if it should, as his March 4 draft did, ask for a specific number of dollars to be used in Greece and also in "Turkey or in such other country as may find itself in need of help maintaining that economic stability necessary to the survival of its independence and free institutions." Because Truman was still in Mexico, the White House had not yet spelled out exactly what it wanted to request, leaving Jones unsure as to how he should proceed. The Public Affairs officer put the question to Acheson on the morning of March 6. According to Jones, "Acheson leaned back, looked over at the White House, thought a while, and said slowly, 'If F.D.R. were alive I think I know what he'd do. He would make a statement of global policy but confine his request for money right now to Greece and Turkey.'" Jones's revision, completed later that day, followed Acheson's advice and was subjected to yet another drafting conference with Acheson and just a few other staff members, where very few changes were recommended.[15]

Upon his return from Baylor, Truman met with Acheson, Clifford, and Snyder. It was at this meeting that the president agreed to the $250 million in aid for Greece and another $150 million in aid for Turkey. The meeting's participants discussed another issue, as well, however: the means by which Truman should present the new policy to the country in order to gain citizen and congressional support. Acheson suggested, based on a recommendation from Jones the day before, that the administration abandon the plan for a radio fireside chat since time for preparing a second message was running low. Acheson and Jones believed that Truman's appearance before a joint session of Congress would be more "impressive" and more in keeping with the forceful nature of the speech. The president agreed and then met with his cabinet to discuss the situation.[16]

After this meeting, Acheson received a cable from Marshall, who was in Paris on his way to Moscow, responding to Jones's March 6 draft. The secretary of state asked for several changes that he considered "highly desirable." First, Marshall asked that Acheson eliminate a phrase that described aggression as a threat to U.S. national security, "regardless of whether effected in the name of Fascism, Nazism or Communism." This request likely reflected the concern that Bohlen attributed to Marshall about the speech sounding too inflammatory towards the Soviet Union, particularly in the midst of the Moscow conference. In addition, the secretary of state wanted the deletion of a paragraph that compared the monarchy of Greece to the monarchy of England, probably because the comparison was neither particularly accurate nor particularly helpful, especially when dealing with American citizens, many of whom held Great Britain in low esteem. Marshall also asked that a line stating, "It [the situation in Greece and Turkey] requires immediate and resolute action" be changed to "The situation, in my opinion, requires immediate and resolute action." The qualifying of the statement was curious, as it undercut the power of the line by transforming it from a statement of fact into a statement of opinion, but Jones dutifully implemented the edit. The last change that Marshall requested was the elimination of a paragraph that insisted funds for Greece and Turkey be made available immediately, because the secretary of state recognized that Congress would not take kindly to such demands.[17]

The White House Gets Involved in Drafting and Editing

Clifford, meanwhile, felt that the White House advisers responsible for speechwriting had been left completely out of the loop. As Elsey wryly observed, "Acheson, never lacking in self-confidence, seemed to think anything he had a hand in needed no input from anyone else." Clifford explicitly had to request a copy of State's latest draft in order to see it. With Elsey's concerns about an "all-out" speech still fresh in his mind, Clifford decided that it would be especially important that the speech contain "no half-steps or ambivalent language." Americans would need to be shocked into understanding and supporting the administration's new foreign policy. Once Jones's draft of March 7—reflecting Marshall's requested changes—arrived, Clifford gave it to Elsey, telling him, "We've got to get this thing in shape for the Boss. Read it tonight and tell me in the morning what you think." According to Elsey, he and Clifford both concluded the State draft was unclear about the larger policy implications and spent too much time discussing Great Britain's economic problems.[18]

After a White House staff meeting on the morning of Saturday, March 8, Clifford privately expressed these concerns to Truman, which led to the White House ultimately taking over the drafting. Clifford, with the president's support, called Acheson to request a meeting with State personnel about the speech. The acting secretary of state sent Jones, along with Carl Humelsine, director of the executive secretariat, to meet with Clifford and Elsey that afternoon. At that meeting, the president's special counsel and his special assistant told Jones and Humelsine that the address's organization was weak, since it started with Greece, went on to the wider situation, and then returned to Greece. Instead, they recommended that the speech build to a climax by flowing from a thorough discussion of Greece, going on to the larger implications, and concluding with the specific request. Clifford also recommended tougher language, particularly in the conclusion. At the top of the March 7 speech draft, Jones wrote, "Stronger Peroration" and, on a notepad, scribbled, "This is a serious task we undertake. It has little to recommend it except that the alternative is even more serious," two lines that would appear, nearly unaltered, in the March 12 address. Jones's annotated copy of the March 7 draft also indicates that Clifford and Elsey suggested places where excess verbiage could be trimmed, a point that must have made an impression on him. Jones's notes on the top of the March 9 draft accounted for the number of words in the document, Truman's quick rate of speech—"120 words [a] minute"—and the length of time that it would take the president to read the speech (nineteen minutes).[19]

After the drafting meeting, Jones returned to his office where he used scissors and a stapler to help him reorder the text; it was, he concluded, "a marked improvement." In addition to the other changes already noted, Jones revised his reference to a quotation by former Secretary of State James Byrnes that appeared in the draft. Clifford had told Jones that the president never quoted other people in his speeches, so Byrnes's name was quickly excised and the phrasing slightly reworked. Borrowing much of his wording from Russell, Jones's March 7 effort read: "The world is not static. The *status quo* is not sacred and unchangeable, but as Secretary Byrnes said a year ago, 'we cannot overlook a unilateral gnawing away at the *status quo*. The United Nations Charter,' said Mr. Byrnes, 'forbids aggression and we cannot allow aggression to be accomplished by coercion or pressure or by subterfuges such as political infiltration.'" In Jones's March 9 draft, the same passage appeared, without attribution, as follows: "The world is not static, and the *status quo* is not sacred. We cannot overlook, however, a unilateral gnawing away at the *status quo*. We cannot allow aggression to be accomplished in violation of the Charter of the United Nations by such methods as coercion, or by such subterfuges as political infiltration."[20] This excerpt, after additional refinement, took its place in the final text.

Jones had his revision, the draft of March 9, in Clifford's and Elsey's hands by Sunday. The two men worked on the speech together that afternoon, reading lines aloud and making adjustments. On Monday morning, March 10, Elsey worked alone from a clean copy, only seen by him and Clifford, which reflected the changes the two men had already made; from this, Elsey created the draft of March 10. An examination of both the March 9 revision and the March 10 draft indicates the influence that Clifford and Elsey had on the speech.

First, they adapted the sentence structure and language to make them more compatible with Truman's style. In their editing, Clifford and Elsey quickly deleted excess verbiage, reducing the length of the section describing the details of Greece's request from five paragraphs to two. Simple words also took the place of more complicated terms, so that "rectified" became "corrected," "expenditure of any funds" became "use of any funds," and "The government of Greece has its imperfections" became "The government of Greece is not perfect." This was routine work for Elsey and Clifford. As Elsey once explained, the two men frequently worked to "depolish" passages contributed by individuals not on staff because their drafts simply did not sound like Truman. Clifford and Elsey also realized that simpler sentences were essential for the president's formal addresses because Truman's poor eyesight made it difficult for him to look down at a text, look up at the audience, and then refocus on the text. The president, Elsey reflected, "did not read well. His delivery was not that of a polished orator when he was reading a formal address. It was just a fact of life. We accepted it. This is what you were working with; you play the cards you're dealt. He did his damnedest, and we did ours." In the Truman Doctrine speech, as they did when preparing other formal addresses, Clifford and Elsey chose to "Trumanize" by simplifying word choices and eliminating complex sentences.[21]

Clifford and Elsey made many other changes, as well. According to Elsey, he was concerned at the time "by the absence of what today would be called 'a sound bite.'" To fix the problem, he kept reworking what appeared to be a key statement, the section that started with "I believe it must be the policy of the United States," which Acheson and Jones had formulated for the March 6 version by combining a line culled from Russell's "Basic United States Policy" with the "I believe" phraseology from Henderson's draft. Elsey eventually broke the paragraph into three separate paragraphs, each of which began with the phrase "I believe." The passage began, "I believe that it must be the policy of the United States to support free peoples who are resisting attempted subjugation by armed minorities or by outside forces." It went on to assert that the United States must help "free peoples to work out their own destinies in their own way" and that U.S. aid should be "primarily" economic in nature. Aside from State's insistence that "pressures" be substituted for "forces" in the first line, Elsey's refashioning of the passage—what he and Clifford referred to as the speech's "credo"—would remain intact and become the best-known and most quoted part of the Truman Doctrine address.[22]

When the March 7 draft of the speech had arrived from State, Clifford had distributed copies to several other members of the administration, too, such as Snyder and Forrestal. In the March 9 revision, he and Elsey added a passage at the behest of Snyder and other conservatives in the cabinet, albeit not with great enthusiasm. The new paragraph began, "There has been a world-wide trend away from the system of free enterprise toward state-controlled economies" and warned of the threat that chaos in other countries posed to both free enterprise and democracy. It concluded, "If we allow systems of free enterprise in other nations to collapse, one by one, to outside pressure, we may soon find ourselves alone in our faith and the very existence of our economy will be threatened." Acheson later insisted that this part be cut since it might limit whom the United States could help, and one of the eventual recipients of U.S. aid might be Great Britain, which had a Labour government. Clifford was quick to agree, so quick in fact that Jones accurately surmised that the changes must have been "suggested by neither him nor the President but by others" in the White House.[23]

Other additions by Clifford and Elsey included references to the Middle East as "an area of great natural resources" that must be accessible to all, which the State Department also later removed, and a paragraph from Humelsine, requested by Elsey, that justified unilateral U.S. action on the grounds that the United Nations was not yet established enough to do the job. That addition would stay, in Elsey's words, to "help placate the critics that we were *certain* we would be having because we were going a non-U.N. route." Both Russell and Jones reflected later that little attention had been paid to the United Nations during the drafting process, despite Russell's emphasis upon the United Nations in the informational themes of "Basic United States Policy." In retrospect, several factors may have led to this outcome. Although the United Nations was young—the first meeting of the General Assembly took place in London in January 1946—the administration likely feared that the Soviets would veto any U.N. action. Additionally, Acheson's own antipathy toward the United Nations may have shaped the early

State drafts. In response to later criticism about the Truman Doctrine bypassing the United Nations, Clifford and Elsey included positive passages about the United Nations in the president's April 1947 Jefferson Day speech, but Acheson tried, unsuccessfully, to have them removed. He told Clifford that the United Nations "had been greatly 'over-played' & 'over-sold,' & that U.N. was not designed to 'prevent wars' & could not 'stop wars'—& that President would be best to omit any reference to U.N." When Clifford shared Acheson's comments with Elsey, his assistant recorded, "I blew my top.... I said Pres. could not ... take a course of ignoring U.N. or announcing it was a 'dead duck'—he has to continue to profess faith in its ultimate success or it really will be dead for all time."[24] Not surprisingly, then, it was Elsey who had seen the need for an additional paragraph about the United Nations, but even this addition would prove too cursory to meet objections.

Finally, one cannot conclude a discussion of Elsey and Clifford's significant changes in the March 9 revision and March 10 draft without pointing out their use of vivid imagery. In their hands, for instance, "the armed depredations of several thousand political dissidents" threatening Greece were transformed into "the terrorist activities of several thousand armed men," words that conveyed a more frightening scene. Clifford and Elsey also added a section to the conclusion of the speech that appealed strongly to pathos, a passage that Jones said Clifford himself contributed to the March 9 version that Jones produced. Although Jones's notes on his March 7 draft indicate that the White House speechwriters may have suggested something along these lines, the passage does not actually appear until the March 9 revised draft reflecting Elsey's and Clifford's edits completed on the afternoon of March 9. Clifford claimed to be the author of the addition, which read: "The seeds of totalitarian regimes are nurtured by misery and want. They spread and grow in the evil soil of poverty and strife. They burst forth in their full stature when the hope of a people for a better life has died. We must keep alive the flame of hope in the Greek people."[25] This passage would later become a point of contention between Clifford and Acheson, but it was a point that Clifford would win.

In view of the vivid scene of crisis that they described, it is also not surprising that Clifford and Elsey strengthened the line that Marshall had qualified. The March 9 revision transformed "The situation, in my opinion, requires immediate and resolute action" into "The situation requires immediate and resolute action." By the March 10 draft, Elsey had settled on "We must take immediate and resolute action," words that emphasized the need for the United States, specifically, to act.[26]

On the morning of Monday, March 10, Elsey took the most recent draft to members of the White House staff, such as Ross and Correspondence Secretary William Hassett, who was considered an excellent wordsmith. Clifford, meanwhile, shared the latest version with Truman. According to Elsey, "This was the first draft shown to HST." The president's late involvement in the specific wording of the message was typical of Truman, who preferred delegating such matters so he could concentrate on other issues. In the case of the Truman Doctrine, the president's trip to Mexico while State was preparing its drafts also served to distance him from the process.[27]

The president, Clifford, Elsey, Ross, and Hassett met on the afternoon of March 10 to go over a speech that already had its content and phrasing largely set. According to Clifford, the usual format for such conferences was for Truman to "read the entire speech aloud to get the whole feel of it and everybody would have a copy and follow along. Then he'd go back and read a paragraph. And at the end of the paragraph he'd stop and different people would make suggestions." Of the usual participants in such meetings, Ross was the one whose voice most often carried the day. The press secretary was a skillful writer and grammarian who had won the 1932 Pulitzer Prize while at the *St. Louis Post-Dispatch* before coming to the White House. Beyond Ross's longtime friendship with Truman, then, the president usually listened to what Ross had to say about wording because, as Elsey once chuckled, "Charlie was invariably right." At the March 10 White House speech conference on the Truman Doctrine address, the president, Clifford, Elsey, Ross, and Hassett primarily worked on tightening up the prose, with Ross eliminating unneeded articles and conjunctions and, in one case, changing passive voice to active voice. The group edited Clifford's addition to the peroration so that the "seeds of totalitarian regimes" would no longer "burst forth in their full stature" but rather "reach their full growth," a reformulation that was more consistent with his metaphor. The men also added language that enhanced the sense of crisis created by the text by emphasizing that only the United States could act and—if it did not—predicting that both world peace and U.S. national security would be endangered.[28]

Although Truman clearly took part in the conference, it is hard to know exactly what he thought of the draft, as most of his sparse longhand comments on it repeated some—but certainly not all—of what White House staffers, particularly Ross, suggested at the White House meeting. The degree to which Truman's notes simply reflected the speech conference discussion he had been part of, or consisted of personal reactions written down before the meeting by a president whose White House staffers were in *simpatico* with him, is hard to say. In addition to comments that paralleled those made by others, Truman wrote "polish" in the margin beside the initial description of Greece and suggested adding "Latvia, Lithuania, and Estonia" as examples of other countries that were under pressure from "totalitarian regimes," a recommendation that was not followed, undoubtedly because it was considered too antagonistic to the Soviet Union. In two places on the text, the president replaced "wish to" and "is" with "shall" and "shall be," respectively, to create stronger constructions; these changes remained in the final draft. Truman's later insistence that he changed "shall" to "must" in the credo section *may* simply have been a mistaken recollection over his edits in regard to the word "shall."[29] Regardless of their brevity, the president's longhand comments are among his few recorded responses to the March 10 version, and Elsey, who carefully noted in the margins of his copy the names of individuals who made significant suggestions for revision, never mentioned Truman once.

After the White House polishing session, Clifford took the marked-up version to the State Department. Acheson and Jones cut the references to free enterprise and to Greece and Turkey's importance in safeguarding access to Middle East oil, as mentioned earlier, and asked for a few other minor changes, as well, most of which they got. Two points were not readily conceded, however. First, State wanted the word "everywhere" inserted into a line on page 12 of the draft so that it would read, "Discouragement and possibly failure would quickly be the lot of neighboring peoples everywhere engaged in a struggle to maintain their freedom and independence." In the margin of Elsey's annotated copy, he wrote, "State puts in 'everywhere'; GME & CMC take it out."[30] Elsey and Clifford, as political advisers to the president, were especially sensitive to adding "everywhere" because it would provide an easy target for isolationist critics, as well as for congressional advocates of China, a government toward which the administration was highly ambivalent as Truman's comment about Chiang Kai-shek in his March 7 cabinet meeting reflected. In the end, Elsey and Clifford succeeded in keeping the word out of the final text.

The other disagreement between the White House and the State Department, as revealed by the annotated drafts, was that Acheson and Jones wanted Clifford's "seeds of totalitarian regimes" addition deleted, but the special counsel was not willing to surrender it. According to Clifford, he thought the State Department draft was "too weak" without some of the "language"—presumably a reference to this section—he had added. Clifford recalled that he and Acheson "had quite a time over the message." Given Acheson's own penchant for dramatic language, his opposition to Clifford's contribution is puzzling. The answer may be that Acheson, based on his earlier communication with Marshall, believed the secretary would disapprove of additional emotional language and, since the words were neither Acheson's nor produced under his guidance at State, he had no personal attachment to them. Ultimately, though, it was the special counsel who had the president's ear. Clifford observed, "I thought that language was sound, President Truman thought it was sound, and that language stayed there."[31]

On Tuesday, March 11, the White House held a final speech conference with Truman, Clifford, Elsey, and the president's entire staff at the regular 9:00 A.M. staff meeting. Truman appears to have been more involved in this session, in part because he was more familiar with the text than he had been at the first speech session and also perhaps because the second session focused on fine-tuning smaller word choices for purpose of delivery. On his annotated copy of the March 11 draft,

Truman made a number of corrections, almost all of which dealt with simplifying word choice, such as replacing "assistance" with "aid" and "assist" with "help." What is significant about these corrections is that Elsey had sometimes already edited his copy in a different way and *then* made changes that matched the edits on the president's draft. In other cases, Elsey's corrected copy does not reflect the changes marked on Truman's copy, but the final copy—the March 11 revision—does. In final speech sessions like this one, Truman characteristically took a more active role in suggesting ways to simplify, and the edits on his annotated copy of the March 11 draft seem consistent with this pattern and with Elsey's assertion that Truman "*always* had the *final* word in editing."[32]

Once the White House had completed its review, Elsey prepared the final copy of the presidential address, which was released to the State Department later that afternoon for its foreign broadcasts. Clifford and then Truman himself would mark up copies to aid the president in his delivery of the speech before Congress the following day. Again, the White House took care to make the speech as easy for Truman to deliver as it could. The reading copy was triple-spaced, with wide margins of two inches on the left and nearly two inches on the right, short paragraphs—often only a sentence long—and conventional capitalization, a format that Truman insisted upon for all of his formal presidential speeches. Finally, the manuscript was placed in the black loose-leaf notebook from which Truman preferred to deliver.[33]

In examining the evolution of the Truman Doctrine speech, one is struck by the immense number of people involved: Henderson, Merriam, Russell, Jones, Acheson, Humelsine, Marshall, Clifford, Elsey, Ross, Hassett, Snyder, Truman, and other countless (and often nameless) State Department and White House officials. Despite past controversies over its authorship—and the not so subtle jockeying for credit that has occasionally taken place among some of the parties—Clifford may have summed up the matter best when he said, "no single person could assert paternity."[34]

What united these individual authors was both the generative force and strategic considerations of rhetoric. While previous messages like the Long Telegram, Churchill's Westminster speech, and the Clifford-Elsey Report had helped forge a common interpretive framework for Soviet behavior among administration officials, not everyone in the United States shared this perception of reality. Hence, White House and State Department officials working on the speech also had to consider carefully persuasive strategies for gaining public and congressional support. Although they may not have been aware of the ways in which past rhetoric had helped generate their own views of the current world situation, the men in the Truman administration were highly conscious of the strategic considerations of the president's words, as Truman's own comment about the need to sell the new foreign policy demonstrated.

On March 12, 1947, Truman went to Capitol Hill and announced his new foreign policy in a speech that promoted a sense of crisis and called on the nation to fulfill its international responsibilities. Several features of the address worked together to present a compelling case: highly structured arguments—infused with a crisis terminology—that employed anticipatory rebuttals, fear appeals, and periodic use of strategic ambiguity; embedded metaphors of disease, violation, and chaos that operated on a less conscious level to induce fear; and an unadorned style and delivery that lent a sense of realism to the president's claims.

Rhetorical Strategy in Truman's Speech

In the Truman Doctrine speech, as in his other presidential rhetoric, Truman's structure was exceedingly clear. He briefly told the audience that his message would deal with Greece and Turkey, as well as U.S. foreign policy and national security. The president then noted that Greece had made an "urgent" plea for aid and that he did not "believe that the American people and the Congress wish to turn a deaf ear to the appeal of the Greek Government." In his post–White House years, Truman would reflect that the speaker he most tried to emulate was Cicero, whose speeches were "models of simplicity and clarity." During their school days in Independence, the president and Charlie Ross had translated Cicero's orations from Latin, and the texts had made a big impression on Truman. Cicero's method was "to state his case and then prove it," Truman said admiringly.[35] Although the president maintained a low degree of involvement in the White House speechwriting process, Clifford and Elsey clearly knew what he wanted. The president was certainly no Cicero, but his structure was typically straightforward and easy to comprehend. Likewise in the Truman Doctrine speech, after briefly establishing his basic thesis, the president supported it in a step-by-step, instructional fashion.

For Truman, the first task was to depict Greece as a sympathetic nation that faced grave danger. The president stated that Greece was an "industrious, peace loving country" whose people "work hard to make both ends meet." Since 1940, he explained, Greece "has suffered invasion, four years of cruel enemy occupation, and bitter internal strife." Truman then detailed the dire state of affairs: the retreating Germans had destroyed the nation's infrastructure and burned more than a thousand villages. Moreover, at the end of the war, "*Eighty-five percent* of the children were tubercular. Livestock, poultry, and draft animals had almost disappeared. Inflation had wiped out practically all savings." According to the president, these "tragic conditions" had led "a militant minority" to exploit the situation, resulting in political instability and an inability to recover economically. No explanation of the composition of this "militant minority" was offered, nor did Truman acknowledge—at this point in the speech—the Greek government's complicity in the political upheaval, nor would he mention here or later the government's own corruption and squandering of funds. Instead, the president focused on what Greece required. "Greece is in desperate need of financial and economic assistance to enable it to resume purchases of food, clothing, fuel and seeds. These are indispensable for the subsistence of its people and are obtainable only from abroad." In addition, Truman said the Greek government had asked for "American administrators, economists, and technicians" to insure that aid was "used effectively."

To underscore the danger that necessitated these requests, the president declared, "The very existence of the Greek state is today threatened by the terrorist activities of *several thousand armed men, led by Communists,* who defy the government's authority," particularly along Greece's border with Albania, Bulgaria, and Yugoslavia. This sentence was the only time in the entire speech that Truman used the word "Communist," while he never mentioned the Soviets or the Soviet Union at all. Nonetheless, the president's reference to Albania, Bulgaria, and Yugoslavia left little doubt about the identity of the Communist culprit that Truman had in mind. He also was careful not to identify the insurgents as Greek, which would have immediately raised questions among Americans about the appropriateness of U.S. involvement in a civil war.

To give further credence to his charges about outside interference in Greece, the president pointed out that a U.N. Commission was investigating "disturbed conditions in northern Greece and alleged border violations" by countries on its northern frontier, a statement that also allowed Truman to tip his hat to the authority of the United Nations. At the same time, though, the president made it clear that help could not wait, for "the Greek Government is unable to cope with the situation. The Greek army is small and poorly equipped." Truman then cut to the chase: "*Greece must have* this assistance if it is to become a *self-supporting* and *self-respecting* democracy. The United States must supply this assistance."

In the next section of his speech, the president anticipated and refuted arguments that he expected critics to make against his assertion that the United States needed to take action. Truman's prepared remarks as president typically employed such maneuvers, what Underhill called his "anticipatory rebuttals for arguments certain to arise." He explained that the relief already provided by the United States to Greece was "inadequate" given the challenge and, additionally, that no other nation, including Great Britain, was strong enough "to provide the necessary support."[36] Truman's counter-arguments here wisely kept the focus on Greece's critical state, rather than emphasizing Great Britain's tribulations.

After eliminating current U.S. aid levels to Greece and aid from other countries as the solutions to Greece's problems, the president attempted to refute the other obvious answer: the United Nations. He stated, "We have considered how the United Nations might assist in this crisis. But the situation is an urgent one requiring immediate action, and the United Nations and its related organizations are not in a position to extend help of the kind that is required." This was the paragraph that Humelsine had sent, at Elsey's request, in anticipation of criticisms about not going through the United Nations. Since Truman had been a major proponent of the United Nations, his proposal that the United States act unilaterally would be troubling to many. Expectations for the United Nations were exceedingly, often unrealistically, high in its early years, but nevertheless the Truman Doctrine speech did not do enough to maintain the institution's legitimacy. Possibly a variation on a second paragraph about the United Nations that Humelsine sent to Elsey would have helped. In that text, Humelsine wrote that the United States was "stepping into the breach" by providing aid to Greece and Turkey "in order to help maintain conditions in which the United Nations can grow in international confidence and authority." The passage noted that the United States had "taken the lead" in creating international agencies to help with postwar reconstruction and concluded, "We will continue to study ways and means through which the United Nations and related international agencies might undertake financial and economic responsibilities in such areas." If Truman had indicated willingness, indeed readiness, to have the United Nations take over the provision of aid to Greece and Turkey once it was able to do so, his speech would have managed the U.N. issue more effectively. He also would have preempted a legislative compromise, orchestrated by Vandenberg to gain successful passage of the aid bill, which permitted the United Nations to end American aid to Greece and Turkey when "action taken or assistance furnished by the United Nations makes the continuance of such assistance unnecessary or undesirable."[37]

Once the president's address removed the United Nations as a potential source of aid, Truman also anticipated two other arguments about Greece itself: that Greece would mismanage U.S. aid and that the reactionary Greek government was not a democracy worthy of American assistance. First, the president repeated his earlier claim that the Greek government wanted U.S. help in "utilizing effectively" the aid provided. He stressed, "It is of the utmost importance that we supervise the use of any funds made available in Greece," a line that prompted a scattering of applause from the budget-conscious Republican Congress. Second, Truman noted, "No government is perfect. One of the chief virtues of a democracy, however, is that its defects are always *visible* and under democratic processes can be pointed out and corrected. The government of Greece is not perfect." He then inflected upward in a tone akin to a schoolteacher, "*Nevertheless* it represents 85 percent of the members of the Greek Parliament who were chosen in an election last year. Foreign observers, including 692 Americans, considered this election to be a fair expression of the views of the Greek people." In this passage, Truman's words established an enthymeme or rhetorical syllogism for the audience to complete.[38] If democracies are imperfect but can be corrected and the Greek government is a democracy, then listeners could clearly infer that the Greek government's defects could be corrected. The president also admitted that the Greek government "has made mistakes," but he justified them as a result of the chaos that existed in Greece. At the same time, Truman clarified, "The extension of aid by *this country* does not mean that the United States condones *everything* that the Greek Government has done or will do. We have *condemned in the past,* and we *condemn now,* extremist measures of the right or the left." When viewed from the vantage point of more than six decades of U.S. presidential crisis and war rhetoric, the president's admission that the Greek government was less than ideal seems refreshingly honest. It served him well at the time by conceding the almost certain criticism that opponents would level and, simultaneously, permitting him to "inoculate" other listeners against such criticisms by providing a defense of the democratic nature of the Greek government and an explanation of the context in which its "mistakes" had taken place. By emphasizing that he did not condone everything the Greek government had done, Truman depicted himself as informed and reasonable.

The president had, by this time in his address, established the danger that Greece faced and why the United States had to help; he had also anticipated and refuted counter-arguments about other countries or the U.N. handling the situation and about the dubious fiscal responsibility and democratic practices of the Greek government. Truman then tackled the task of establishing Turkey's need for U.S. assistance, a most challenging undertaking since Turkey was not exactly a poster child for international sympathy. During World War II, Turkey had studiously refused the Allies' repeated requests that it join in fighting the Axis powers; hence, Turkey had escaped the ravages of war that engulfed Greece. Turkey's government was also far from what most people would conceive as a democracy. In fact, one of the reasons that Kennan opposed the Truman Doctrine as it evolved into policy in an early speech draft was because he objected to Turkey receiving aid of any kind. On the morning that Truman delivered his address, even Secretary of War Patterson stated his opposition to military aid to Turkey and agreed to it only when Acheson pointed out that the president had already approved both economic and military assistance to the country.[39] The Truman Doctrine speech attempted to manage such perceptions of Turkey in several ways.

First, the president spent most of his time talking about Greece, whose situation made for a more compelling case, instead of talking about Turkey. Of the initial twenty-eight paragraphs of the Truman Doctrine address, for instance, eighteen focused exclusively on Greece's problems or the provision of aid to Greece. Conversely, only four paragraphs dealt solely with Turkey, and each was a mere sentence in length. Four other paragraphs—the longest only four sentences long—discussed Greece and Turkey together.

A second tactic that Truman employed was, again, to anticipate critics by conceding that Turkey was in a better position than Greece but then to justify the extension of aid to Turkey through its association with Greece and through vague references to the preservation of order. According to the president, "The circumstances in which Turkey finds itself today are considerably different from those of Greece. Turkey has been spared the disasters that have beset Greece. And during the war, the United States and Great Britain furnished Turkey with material aid." The truth was that Turkey, more so than Greece, was a point of strategic interest to the United States because of the Black Sea Straits, but Truman's speech did not acknowledge this fact. Rather, the president linked the fate of Turkey to that of Greece by discussing Turkey immediately after Greece in the speech and emphasizing their commonality. For example, Truman transitioned to Turkey with, "Greece's neighbor, Turkey, also deserves our attention," a sentence that suggested Turkey's proximity both to Greece and to Greece's perils.

However, the president provided no real explanation of the specific hazards that Turkey faced, particularly in comparison to the detailed narrative that he told in establishing Greece's vulnerability. After Truman admitted that Turkey was in less danger than its neighbor, he immediately followed his admission with the same teacher-like upward inflection that he had employed in his defense of Greece as a democracy, adding, "*Nevertheless,* Turkey now needs our support." The president declared, "Since the war Turkey has sought additional financial assistance from Great Britain and the United States for the purpose of effecting that modernization necessary for the maintenance of its national integrity. That integrity is essential to the preservation of order in the Middle East." While these words sounded impressively foreboding, they explained little about why Turkey needed aid or modernization. Truman concluded the section by saying that Great Britain could no longer help Turkey and, "As in the case of Greece, if Turkey is to have the assistance it needs, the United States must supply it." While the president was clear about what he wanted done, he was comparatively hazy about *why* it had to be done.

Admittedly, Turkey was a difficult case to make. Jones explained that the State Department also feared the American public would reject a policy based on strategic military considerations in peacetime. Given how readily Clifford agreed to Acheson's request to delete a reference in the speech to protecting access to Middle East oil, it appears at least some individuals in the White House agreed with State's perspective. The president's address instead used Greece as a way to gain acceptance on Turkey. As a result, Jones admitted there was "a grain of truth" in what one witness later said about the Truman Doctrine before the House Committee on Foreign Affairs: "It almost appears that when the new dish was being prepared for American consumption, Turkey was slipped into the oven with Greece because that seemed to be the surest way to cook a tough bird."[40]

In his speech, Truman closed the section on Turkey's need for aid by emphatically concluding, *"We are the only country able to provide that help."* On newsreel footage, one can discern a soft, troubled murmuring from the crowd. The president, as if to reassure, then acknowledged that he was "fully aware" of the "broad implications" of his proposed policy and, providing yet another explicit transition, said, "I shall discuss these implications with you at this time."

According to Truman, "One of the primary objectives of the foreign policy of the United States is the creation of conditions in which we and other nations will be able to work out a way of life *free* from coercion." This declaration reflected well both the president's allegiance to Wilsonian idealism and to a new American role in the world. Almost thirty years earlier—April 2, 1917, to be exact—Woodrow Wilson had addressed Congress about the war with Germany, insisting that the United States would fight "for the rights of nations great and small and the privilege of men everywhere to choose their way of life and of obedience. The world must be made safe for democracy."[41] Like Wilson, Truman argued that the desire to protect freedom of choice in government sometimes demanded that the United States use its power: "This was a fundamental issue in the war with Germany and Japan. Our victory was won over countries which sought to impose their will, and their way of life, upon other nations." Through this statement, the president not only lent legitimacy to the tenet he had articulated by associating it with the war effort, but also legitimized the idea that the United States must exert itself to fulfill such an objective.

Truman then established that the application of American power could come in many forms: "To ensure the peaceful development of nations, free from coercion, the United States has taken a leading part in establishing the United Nations. The United Nations is designed to make possible lasting freedom and independence for all its members. We shall *not realize* our objectives, however, unless we are willing to help *free peoples* to *maintain* their *free institutions* and their *national integrity* against *aggressive movements* that seek to impose upon them *totalitarian regimes.* [applause] This is no more than a frank recognition that totalitarian regimes imposed upon free peoples by direct or indirect aggression, undermine the foundations of international peace and hence the security of the United States." This passage was significant for several reasons. First, it heightened the importance of protecting free nations by linking such acts to the preservation of both world peace and U.S. national security. Second, Truman laid the groundwork here for viewing aid to Greece, Turkey, and, one might infer, other countries as simply one more tool for fulfilling a major objective of U.S. foreign policy. Just as going to war against fascism and helping to found the United Nations were useful avenues for obtaining a foreign policy objective—Wilson, too, had engaged in similar endeavors with World War I and the League of Nations—the president indicated that issuing additional foreign aid, like that requested by Greece and Turkey, was a productive policy, as well. This same paragraph, however, undercut the administration's decision to act unilaterally. If the United Nations were "designed to make possible lasting freedom and independence for all its members," then many in the audience may have wondered why Truman had chosen to go around the United Nations. True, he had briefly noted earlier that the United Nations was not yet ready to undertake such a task, but repetition of this idea here and an elaboration elsewhere would have helped immensely.

Finally, Truman made clear that threats to freedom came not just from nation states per se but from "aggressive movements" that sought to impose "totalitarian regimes." His earlier reference to Communists pointed to the identity of such movements, while the applause in response to this particular line indicated that many members of his congressional audience also perceived a Communist threat. The decision to refer to Communists only once in the speech and to the Soviets not at all had its origins with Acheson. Back when planning for the information campaign first began, he directed that administration messages "should not talk provocatively" and, instead, "should avoid accusing the Soviet Union directly." Acheson may have particularly appreciated the relevance of this point after a recent flap in which he himself had been embroiled. In mid-February, the under secretary of state had appeared in a Senate hearing on Lilienthal's nomination as chair of the Atomic Energy Commission. Senator McKellar, vehemently opposed to Lilienthal and attempting to paint him as soft on Communism, had pointedly asked Acheson, "Don't you think Russia would have seized the rest of Europe and the world if she had the atom bomb?" Acheson had tersely replied, "I am quite aware of the fact that Russian foreign policy is an aggressive and expanding one," a statement that Soviet Foreign Minister Molotov pounced on as "a gross slander and hostile to the Soviet Union." Although the controversy eventually blew over, it was undoubtedly on Acheson's mind. Ayers later observed, with almost childlike glee, that the benefit of "totalitarian" was that it left the Soviets "no opening for complaint for if they charge that the reference is to them the reply could be that they admit they are totalitarian."[42] In sum, then, the substitution of less specific terms for the enemy was rhetorically expedient, for most members of Truman's national and international audiences knew to whom he was referring, yet the swap provided the administration with plausible deniability. The substitutions retained much of the anxiety-arousing power of the original names for those who feared the Soviet Union and Communism *because* they understood the code, while less knowledgeable listeners may well have found the idea of nameless aggressive movements imposing totalitarianism around the globe to be a most terrifying specter.

After establishing the objective of protecting freedom and the precedent of acting through a variety of means to fulfill it, the president depicted a frightening world in which more and more free people "have recently had totalitarian regimes forced upon them against their will." He noted, "The Government of the United States has made frequent protests against coercion and intimidation, in violation of the Yalta agreement, in Poland, Rumania, and Bulgaria." This line had the virtue of supporting Truman's assertion, but it also had the unintended impact of confirming right-wing criticisms that the administration had been "soft" at Yalta and in response to Soviet moves in Eastern Europe. When Truman added that "similar developments" had occurred in "a number of other countries," his words conveyed an uncertain future in which nations all over the world were falling to totalitarianism.

Indeed, the president's speech heightened the atmosphere of crisis when he intoned, "At the present moment in world history, nearly every nation must choose between alternative ways of life. The choice is too often not a free one." The word "crisis," ironically enough, derives from the Greek term κρίσις, which means a choosing, a dispute, an issue, or a decision.[43] In his words here, Truman portrayed a world in which almost every country faced a critical decision that would impact its people's entire way of life. The prospect of such a choice would be pressure enough for most, but the president increased tension even more by warning that too many nations were no longer free to make the decision that they desired. Truman's qualifier of "nearly every" nation permitted the possibility that some countries might not have to choose, yet the overall effect of his words was to depict a momentous decision that one could not avoid. Furthermore, the president divided the world into two camps and suggested that countries must choose to join one or the other, for no other alternatives were available.

In the first way of life, Truman expressed, the majority rules with "free institutions, representative government, free elections, guarantees of individual liberty, freedom of speech and religion, and freedom from political oppression." In contrast, the second way of life "is based upon the will of a minority forcibly imposed upon the majority. It relies upon terror and oppression, a controlled press and radio, fixed elections, and the suppression of personal freedoms." Given these alternatives, there is little doubt that most listeners would willingly choose the first way of life. Truman's warnings about aggressive movements forcibly imposing totalitarian regimes around the globe also starkly proposed that the minority in control of the second way of life posed a threat to the majority who chose or wished to choose the first.

After presenting this dichotomy, the president paused and then delivered his credo:

> *I believe* that it must be the policy of the United States to support *free peoples* who are resisting attempted subjugation by *armed minorities* or by outside pressures.
> [pause]

I believe that we must assist *free peoples* to work out their own destinies in their own way.

[pause]

I believe that our help should be primarily through economic and financial aid which is essential to economic stability and orderly political processes.

This section would become the most memorable passage from the Truman Doctrine speech. In *The Cold War as History,* however, Halle would criticize its prose as "inappropriate and weak" because the repeated "I believe" made Truman sound like "a private citizen putting forward a proposal for the consideration of the authorities," rather than the president of the United States.[44] Halle was correct that most formal presidential remarks tend to avoid qualifying phrases of this nature—"I think" or "I believe"—because they cast doubts as to whether a president's words represent reality or simply his opinion of reality, and most presidents prefer not to risk criticisms of their assertions in this way.

In the case of the Truman Doctrine speech, however, the credo that Elsey fashioned for the president was rhetorically effective for several reasons. First, the passage distilled the Truman Doctrine into three simply worded sentences that the audience could easily follow. The text's eloquence also derived from what rhetorical scholars would call anaphora, a stylistic device that is pleasing to the ear because it repeats the same phrase at the beginning of successive clauses.[45] Truman's pauses before each line and stress upon "I believe" added to the appeal by emphasizing the words that followed the repetitive phrase. Lastly, the passage worked because it truly functioned as a credo for the man reciting it. For over a year, Truman had remained publicly silent on his views of the Soviet Union, even as increasing numbers of individuals from the administration, Congress, and the press had come to see Stalin and Communism as threats. Fourteen days had also passed, from the time that Marshall first spoke off the record with reporters about the Greek crisis, with no official message from the president. Although the State Department had blanketed print and radio journalists with messages conducive to the administration's point of view, pressure had been building for Truman himself to speak. The "I believe" section of the Truman Doctrine speech *was* the president's credo, finally committing him publicly to a set of foreign policy principles and indicating the direction in which the nation as a whole should head. Since a credo, by its nature, expresses a philosophy or way of life, the Truman Doctrine's credo seemed particularly appropriate as the president attempted to define and identify with one way of life and to depict it as opposed to another. For all of these reasons, the credo drew the audience's attention to Truman's key ideas in a memorable and compelling fashion.

This does not mean that the credo had no weaknesses, however. Decades later, critics would point to the first line of the passage as evidence for how Truman unleashed a foreign policy that eventually led to the arms race and military interventions in Korea, Vietnam, and elsewhere.[46] Others, including those involved with drafting the speech, would insist that the Doctrine was never intended to apply uniformly around the world, a claim that archival records from the Truman administration support. As both Clifford and Acheson pointed out, the under secretary of state was explicit in his congressional testimony after the address that U.S. support of aid requests from other countries would be decided on a case-by-case basis. The administration did not want congressional supporters of China to push for the policy's application there. For his part, Elsey emphasized that the reason he and Clifford had removed the word "everywhere" from a passage later in the speech was to *avoid* perceptions of universal application. Besides, he added, the last line of the credo said that aid should be primarily economic, so those who interpreted it otherwise were simply wrong.[47]

Several factors account for the disparity of perceptions as to what the credo, the heart of the Truman Doctrine, meant. First, Clifford and Elsey may have removed "everywhere" from the line, "Discouragement and possibly failure would quickly be the lot of neighboring peoples [everywhere] striving to maintain their freedom and independence," but that line did not come until later in the speech and, more importantly, they had not made clear in the credo itself that the principle would apply in only some cases. As one may recall, Henderson's initial draft had qualified the application of U.S. help to other nations: "I, furthermore, firmly believe that the United States must be prepared to give similar assistance to other democratic countries who may require our aid in order to preserve their independence, *particularly when it is clear that the preservation of their independence is important to the interests of the United States*" (emphasis added). Acheson and Jones had drawn on Henderson's writing, merging it with Russell's formulation of "Basic United States Policy" and making the principle more sweeping, perhaps because Henderson's focus on strategic interests seemed less compelling for an American audience and also might prompt questions about the criteria by which U.S. national interests would be decided. Clifford and Elsey's final version of the first line of the credo—"I believe that it must be the policy of the United States to support free peoples who are resisting attempted subjugation by armed minorities or by outside pressures"—continued to encourage listeners to interpret the Doctrine as universal because the sentence contained no qualifiers. After reading a version of this unqualified line in an earlier draft, Under Secretary of the Navy John Sullivan had recommended to Forrestal that the paragraph be reworded to avoid the impression of universal application.[48] Although Clifford received Sullivan's suggestion, subsequent revisions did not act on it.

Another factor that led people to think of the Truman Doctrine in military terms had to do with the ordering of the credo and the fallacies of human attention. Although the third line of the section stated that aid should be primarily economic, it was—after all—the third line, not the first or even the second. Elsey's goal in writing the credo was for something akin to a sound bite. He succeeded, but listeners latched onto the initial sentence and quickly overlooked the third, particularly in light of the frightening context provided by the rest of the speech. Finally, one cannot overlook the fact that the bulk of the aid to Greece did, in fact, turn out to be of a military nature, which prompted political leaders in the future to view the Truman Doctrine in this light.[49] The credo contributed to the compelling nature of the president's speech, then, but the passage also exhibited characteristics that would, in the long term, have unintended consequences, particularly as the Doctrine was put into practice.

After Truman delivered the credo of his speech, he turned again to the United Nations. The president said that the use of "coercion" and "political infiltration" to bring down free nations violated the U.N. Charter. By "helping free and independent nations to maintain their freedom," he expressed, the United States would actually be "giving effect to the principles of the Charter of the United Nations." This passage, once more, raised troubling questions about the United Nations and the U.S. government's relationship to it. If the United Nations were intended to deal with international conflicts, such as those posed by aggressive movements that threatened free nations and violated the U.N. Charter, then why was the United States acting unilaterally? On the other hand, if the United Nations were not strong enough to enforce its own charter, listeners might well wonder how it could handle anything.

Truman followed the touchstone of the U.N. Charter with a passage that connected the fate of Greece and Turkey to the broader state of affairs he had described, portraying a crisis of major proportions that demanded U.S. action. According to the president, "It is necessary only to glance at a map to realize that the survival and integrity of the Greek nation *are of grave importance* in a much wider situation. If Greece should fall under the control of an armed minority, the effect upon its neighbor, Turkey, would be immediate and serious. *Confusion* and *disorder* might well spread throughout the entire Middle East." Truman told how the domino effect of Greece's fall would reach Europe where it would jeopardize countries struggling to recover from World War II. Moreover, he warned, "Collapse of free institutions and loss of independence would be disastrous not only for them but for the world. Discouragement and *possibly failure* would quickly be the lot of neighboring peoples striving to maintain their freedom and independence. Should we fail to aid Greece and Turkey in this fateful hour, the effect will be *far reaching* to the West as well as to the East." Truman's speech had earlier made the case for assistance to Greece and Turkey. Afterward, he had detailed a horrific trend of aggressive movements imposing totalitarian regimes all around the world. In this section of his address, he linked the two, arguing vividly how the failure to help Greece and Turkey could mean the end of freedom for other countries and, the president implied, perhaps for the United States itself. He concluded, "We must take *immediate* and *resolute action*."

Now that Truman had done what he could to ready his audience to act, he made his specific requests of Congress: $400,000,000 in aid for Greece and Turkey; American civilian and military personnel to help with reconstruction and "for the purpose of supervising the use of such financial and material assistance as may be furnished"; training for "selected Greek and Turkish personnel"; and "authority which will permit the speediest and most effective use, in terms of needed commodities, supplies, and equipment, of such funds as may be authorized." Through the president's call for U.S. personnel to oversee aid to Greece and Turkey, he underscored again the fiscally responsible nature of the assistance program, as he did with his request for authority to allow the "most effective use" of that aid. Truman also told legislators that he would come to them if "further funds, or further authority" were needed, and he emphasized how important it was that the White House and Congress work together on the issue at hand.

Interestingly, although the president alluded to how the "Greek army is small and poorly equipped," he explicitly mentioned help of a military nature only once: in his request for personnel who could assist in reconstruction and oversight. Yet, the actual Greek aid program would be mostly military, including motor vehicles, ammunition, weapons, and even American advisors in the field. Likewise, Turkey would be the recipient of extensive military aid that would complete, in just three years time, the training of over nineteen thousand Turkish officers and enlisted men in U.S.-run courses in Turkey, the United States, and Germany.[50] While Truman and his advisors could not have anticipated every need that would arise, they certainly knew in March 1947 that the bulk of Greek-Turkish aid would be military in character. Nevertheless, the Truman Doctrine speech was careful to speak of the proposed assistance in ways that were neutral ("aid," "assistance") or in ways that emphasized its economic and humanitarian dimensions

("economic and financial aid," "certain types of relief and economic aid," and "financial and economic assistance . . . to resume purchases of food, clothing, fuel and seeds.")

The president chose to be strategically ambiguous for two reasons. First, Americans had just been through a terrible war. Neither citizens nor most members of Congress were prepared to risk another military conflict. If Truman had emphasized the military nature of the proposed aid, his domestic audience may well have rebelled, fearing that our intervention would lead to another war. A government-commissioned survey conducted a few weeks after the president's speech confirmed such concerns. Although the Survey Research Center at the University of Michigan found "a sizeable majority" of Americans were in favor of sending economic aid to Greece, it informed the administration that citizens did not approve of military assistance because it "might involve us in war."[51] A second reason for discussing aid in strategically ambiguous ways was that the president, too, wanted to avoid provoking Stalin unnecessarily. Truman did not want war any more than other Americans did, but he also had concluded—in contrast to his hero, Wilson—that power was the ultimate arbiter in international relations. The president believed Greece and Turkey needed military assistance for the West to achieve the balance of power necessary to stop Soviet aggression. While Truman had every intention of giving it to them, he and his administration saw no need to alarm the Soviets and risk war by emphasizing the military character of much of the proposed aid.

After the president finished making his specific request of Congress, he attempted to clinch the deal. Truman conceded that his proposal marked a momentous shift in U.S. policy but warned that doing nothing would have ominous consequences. He said, "This is a *serious course* upon which we embark. I would *not* recommend it except that the *alternative* is *much more serious.*" As the president started his next sentence, belated applause erupted. He paused a few seconds and began anew, once more connecting assistance for Greece and Turkey to World War II and the larger foreign policy objective of protecting freedom, while at the same time underscoring the proposed policy's fiscal restraint. Truman instructed, "The United States contributed $341,000,000,000 toward winning World War II. This is an investment in world free-dom and world peace. The assistance that I am recommending for Greece and Turkey amounts to little more than 1/10 of 1 percent of this investment. It is *only* common sense that we should safeguard *this investment* and make sure that it was *not in vain*." In early 1947, Elsey had helped prepare a memorandum for Leahy on the cost of the war; Truman's use of the figure marked its first public release. Even though the memorandum also included information on the cost of the war in terms of casualties, Elsey had wisely chosen not to include that figure.[52] Mention of the war's financial outlay framed the discussion as a practical cost-benefit analysis, while the phrase "make sure that it was not in vain"—frequently used in regard to lives lost in war—subtly invoked the nation's greater sacrifice without raising war fears to a fever pitch or giving the president the appearance of exploiting war dead for his own political ends.

Truman then drew on Clifford and Elsey's improved peroration to remind his audience one last time of the dangers that the enemy posed and the importance that the United States act:

> The seeds of totalitarian regimes are nurtured by misery and want. They spread and grow in the evil soil of poverty and strife. They reach their full growth when the hope of a people for a better life has died.
>
> *We* must keep that hope alive.
>
> The free peoples of the world look to us for support *in maintaining their freedoms.*
>
> If we falter in our leadership, we may endanger the peace of the world—and we shall surely endanger the welfare of this Nation.

The president's words articulated a crucial role for the United States that was new, but his rhetoric also reflected a sense of American exceptionalism that was as old as the Puritans. In this passage, Truman additionally blended American idealism with American self-interests such that one was virtually indistinguishable from the other: by helping others, we helped ourselves, and by helping ourselves, we helped others. According to McMahon, this theme would become a consistent feature of Truman's foreign policy rhetoric and the Cold War rhetoric of the presidents who followed.[53] The president's words also indicated that acting now to help Greece and Turkey could prevent war rather than instigate it. Truman ended his speech by suggesting that there was little time to deliberate and that it was external crises, not he, pressing the United States to involve itself more extensively in world affairs. As Truman counseled, "Great responsibilities have been placed upon us by the swift movement of events." He then closed, "I am confident that the Congress will face these responsibilities squarely," a line that simultaneously flattered the legislative branch and held it accountable for the security of both the country and the entire free world.

Taken as a whole, the Truman Doctrine speech relied heavily upon highly structured arguments that helped listeners follow the president's line of thought. Interspersed were words that conveyed a sense of crisis, such as "urgent appeal," "fateful hour," and "swift movement of events." In making his arguments, Truman anticipated and refuted counter-arguments that he reasonably could expect, heightened a sense of crisis through fear appeals ("aggressive movements," "terrorist activities," "totalitarian regimes imposed upon free peoples," "every nation must choose"), and, in regard to Turkey and the type of aid he proposed for both countries, employed strategic ambiguity.

Embedded Metaphors in Truman's Speech

The persuasive appeal of the president's speech operated on a less conscious level, as well, though, because of its use of embedded metaphors. While people typically consider metaphors to be ornamental devices of rhetoric, the conceptual system through which we think, speak, and act is also metaphorical in character. For example, the concepts of down and up operate metaphorically to convey particular meanings: "She came down with a virus" and "His reputation is falling fast" imply illness or weakness; conversely, "He's up and about" and "She rose to the top" convey health and vigor. As Gregg explained, meanings such as these derive from "our bodily experience as it interacts with our environment." People who are seriously ill must lie down, whereas healthy people can stand. Because embedded metaphors draw so little attention to themselves, they often shape our perceptions without our conscious awareness. Beer and Landtsheer observed that metaphors may become "so sedimented through time and use that we employ them unawares, draw on their accumulated cultural capital for persuasive power. They are like enthymemes, relying on the audience's knowledge of the missing term of the argument. They blindly and effortlessly move on an ocean of convention, conformity, majority usage, habit and opinion until they are called out."[54] In the Truman Doctrine speech, embedded metaphors enhanced the president's persuasive appeals *because* they were so ordinary and therefore shaped perceptions in ways that members of the audience and even the administration who employed them were most likely unaware.

First, Truman's address frequently drew upon embedded metaphors of health and disease. He claimed that Greece was "unable" to cope and worried about whether it could *"survive"* as a free nation and develop an economy where a *"healthy* democracy can *flourish."* In his speech, the president also vocally emphasized the percentage of Greek children who were tubercular, a literal fact that nonetheless worked in tandem with his embedded disease metaphors. Truman argued that aid was essential for the *"bare subsistence"* and "recovery" of Greece and to keep Turkey "sound." If the United States did not provide aid, he warned that Greece would "fall," leading to the "collapse of free institutions," for totalitarianism flourished where "the hope of a people for a better life has died." As to why the United States had to act, Truman insisted that no other country was willing and *"able."* Of course, the president's embedded metaphors of disease were not unique to him. Rather, they were part of the rhetorical stockpile of anti-Communist appeals that existed in the United States long before World War II and that had been evident more recently in the language choices of both administration officials like Acheson and White House opponents like Dirksen, but their power also derived from their conventional use in everyday language. In the world of the

Truman Doctrine speech, the United States was healthy—at least for now—but Communism or totalitarianism was akin to a virus that could infect, weaken, and even destroy freedom and free nations. The natural implication, Ivie concluded, was that Truman's speech "prompted arguments for aiding afflicted nations before an epidemic of communism could spread to the United States."[55] As the president warned at the end of his speech, not acting would endanger our own nation's "welfare." The fact that Truman himself struggled to convey an image of personal health, despite his illness at the time, may have made these embedded metaphors of disease and health particularly compelling to him personally.

A related set of metaphors in the Truman Doctrine address relied upon the fear of violation. Beyond noting border "violations" in northern Greece, Truman spoke of how Germany and Japan had attempted to "impose their will, and their way of life, upon other nations" and how other countries "have recently had totalitarian regimes forced upon them against their will." The president accused aggressive movements of engaging in "political infiltration." To protect freedom, Truman said that the United States must help Turkey maintain its "national integrity" and also help *free peoples* to *maintain* their *free institutions* and their *national integrity* against *aggressive movements* that seek to impose upon them *totalitarian regimes.*" Indeed, the president's speech depicted freedom as frail and in need of protection, for it was freedom and free institutions that were threatened more than Greece, Turkey, and other countries per se. Since freedom often has traditionally feminine connotations—Lady Liberty, for example—its need for protection in Truman's address and in other U.S. Cold War rhetoric may not be surprising, while the feminized threat of violation assumes additional fearful connotations. Embedded metaphors of disease and violation also are related because both rely upon what Chilton described as a container image where "the body is perceived as a container and disease [or other danger] as something that breaks into that boundary."[56] Through such embedded metaphors, Cold War rhetoric like Truman's prompted fear by tapping into fundamental understandings of bodily threats.

A last set of embedded metaphors prominent in the Truman Doctrine address dealt with chaos and order. As the president described it, Greece was threatened because a "militant minority ... was able to create political chaos" or "an atmosphere of chaos" and to "defy the government's authority." He explained that a U.N. Commission was investigating "disturbed conditions" in northern Greece. If Greece and then Turkey succumbed to turmoil, Truman predicted, "*Confusion* and *disorder* might well spread throughout the entire Middle East." The only solution was to help Greece so that it could "restore internal order and security" and "restore authority to the government." In addition, the United States needed to assist Turkey because it was "essential to the *preservation of order* in the Middle East." Aid to free peoples resisting totalitarianism was likewise crucial for "economic stability and orderly political processes." Throughout his speech, Truman depicted an enemy that created chaos and disorder that, in turn, threatened "international peace and hence the security of the United States." The desire for order also has its roots in human experience, for human beings constantly encounter overwhelming amounts of sensory stimulation. To manage this massive data, people impose order. A woman focuses on her radio news program, for example, rather than giving all the sounds in her vicinity—chirping birds, passing cars, rustling leaves, laughing voices—equal degrees of consideration. Or, individuals may perceive larger patterns (a painting of the seashore) that allow them to handle incalculable bits of sensory stimulation (thousands of individual brush strokes). Through methods like these, humans attempt to avoid the nerve-wracking chaos that sensory stimulation can otherwise bring.[57] The fear of disorder, like the fear of disease and violation, is rooted in human experience. In the Truman Doctrine speech and in the presidential Cold War rhetoric that followed, these embedded metaphors had something in common, for the way to avoid chaos, disease, and violation was to protect containers or free nations as they currently existed. Preserving order was akin to protecting health and bodily integrity because it provided security from the fears of chaos, disease, and violation. And as the excerpts in this chapter indicate, Truman heightened the persuasive impact of these embedded metaphors through his tendency to emphasize them vocally as he spoke.

Style and Delivery in Truman's Speech

Although the president was not an eloquent speaker, Underhill once observed, "Truman seemed to win the important arguments." In the case of the Truman Doctrine speech, oddly enough, Truman's simple style and lackluster delivery may actually have enhanced his persuasive appeal. As his explicit structure and occasional schoolteacher inflections suggest, the president tended to take a pedagogical approach to persuasion. He avoided fancy words and rhetorical flourishes, focusing instead on educating his audiences through explanation as a means of persuasion. As noted earlier, Truman's plain style in language choice not only was a personal preference but also a necessity in formal addresses because of his poor eyesight. The president combined this unadorned style with a delivery that was far from ideal, for his voice was nasal in quality, and he often looked down and lost his place.[58] In the Truman Doctrine speech, for instance, the president momentarily stumbled over his words on four different occasions. Newsreel footage of part of the speech shows Truman rarely looked at the audience and, when he did so, maintained his gaze for no more than two seconds at a time. His body was rigid, usually with both hands resting on the podium. Nonetheless, Truman's delivery, paired with his plain pedagogical style, enhanced the credibility of his structured crisis arguments and embedded metaphors by giving him the appearance of one who was simply facing facts or "telling it like it is."[59]

On the occasion of the joint session, the president's illness and weariness were also visible, but these, too, inadvertently aided his effort. Truman's face was drawn, his voice was slightly hoarse, and he had to clear his throat several times during the speech. Still, the president continued to plow through his structured arguments and anticipatory rebuttals, conveying the impression of a reluctant rhetor resigned to sharing bad news. In his explanations, Truman further encouraged such perceptions when he referred to the need to help free peoples as a "frank recognition" of how the world works and when he admitted that he would prefer not to recommend a change in policy, but "the *alternative* is *much more serious.*" The "anti-rhetorical" style and delivery of Truman's speech, then, were actually highly rhetorical, in the same way that realism, as a form of discourse, relies on "brief, clear, and plausible" accounts to argue that the audience must "see things as they are rather than as we would want them to be" if the nation is to succeed.[60] Despite Truman's weaknesses as a speaker, his delivery worked hand in hand with his plain style to enhance his credibility. Together, they created a context in which the president's anticipatory rebuttals and fear appeals seemed quite believable and in which his strategic ambiguity and embedded metaphors were more likely to go unnoticed.

Conclusion

To understand the Truman Doctrine, one must examine power, but one also must examine words. Words generated perceptions of reality, often without the awareness of those who used them, and words were employed to attain strategic goals, persuading in both intentional and unintentional ways. After the war ended in 1945, the Soviets had periodically engaged in behavior that legitimately raised questions among American officials about the motives of their wartime ally. Simultaneously, Kennan's Long Telegram, Churchill's Westminster address, the Clifford-Elsey Report, and other messages had gradually narrowed the framework of possible interpretations of Soviet behavior until, by the time the British notes arrived, the Truman administration had come to view the Soviet Union as an aggressive, expansionistic threat motivated almost entirely by ideology. Words continued to play a central role as policy and information officers at the State Department worked together to articulate the new policy, establishing frames of reference and lines of argument to be used in congressional consultations and news management in order to create a favorable context. Simultaneously, countless State and White House officials drafted and redrafted a possible presidential message, frequently revising in light of persuasive goals and political constraints, occasionally arguing over what words should or should not be included, and—in the White House—editing with the plain style of the president in mind. Once Truman gave voice to the completed text, its words became his words. The structured arguments made his case explicitly, while the embedded metaphors worked on an implicit level. All the while, the president's style and delivery lent credibility to the frightening narrative he told. It had taken many individuals and many words to get there, but the Truman Doctrine came down to the words of just one man. In the end, though, the Truman Doctrine speech would have implications for millions.

CHAPTER 5

Reflections on the Truman Doctrine Speech

As the president ended his address, applause rang out in the House Chamber, more somber than enthusiastic in tone, while the audience rose to its feet in accordance with custom.[1] Truman closed the black notebook that contained his speech, took a drink from the water glass to his right in order to relieve his throat, and looked at his listeners. He nodded soberly to someone in the crowd but seemed ill at ease, perhaps a combination of stress and the seriousness of the event, for there was still no way to know what Congress would do. In just a few minutes, Truman would board a plane for Key West and his delayed vacation.

The night before he delivered the Truman Doctrine speech, the president and First Lady had attended a benefit showing of *The Best Years of Our Lives,* a film that movingly dramatized the efforts of three World War II veterans to adjust to postwar life. Truman, in his own way, had also struggled with the postwar world as he strained for almost two years to make sense of Soviet behavior. Once he had decided, however, the president characteristically did not look back. He wrote to his daughter from Florida, "This terrible decision I had to make had been over my head for about six weeks," an admission that not only spoke to his own conflicting impulses but also revealed that the administration had anticipated the British withdrawal sooner than the February 21 diplomatic notes that Acheson later described as "shockers." In the end, Truman told Margaret, "The attempt of Lenin, Trotsky, Stalin et al., to fool the world and the American Crackpots Association, represented by Jos. Davies, Henry Wallace, Claude Pepper and the actors and artists in immoral Greenwich Village, is just like Hitler's and Mussolini's so-called socialist states. Your Pop had to tell the world just that in polite language."[2]

Reactions to the Truman Doctrine Speech

As the president rested in Key West, the world responded to his address. The reactions overseas were predictably mixed. *Pravda* declared, "beneath the mask of benevolence" in Truman's speech, "there is [a] visible policy of imperialist expansion." Conversely, Churchill proclaimed, "If such a step had been taken by the U.S. before the last war, it would have stopped it." Overall, the Intelligence Division of the War Department may have summed up global responses best: "The Communist line accuses the United States of imperialism that will undermine the United Nations. The moderate, middle-of-the-road groups are generally apprehensive and express fear of what may result. The right-wingers are jubilant."[3]

Meanwhile in the United States, telegrams poured into the White House, most of them supportive, from both ordinary citizens and from public figures like Alf Landon and Douglas Fairbanks. U.S. print and radio coverage was also very positive. Of 225 newspaper editorials received at the White House in the five days after Truman's address, for example, more than half were "100%" in favor of his request, while only 13 completely opposed the president. American media coverage also tended to use language much like Truman's to depict the world situation. For example, the *New York Times* reported that the president "proposed that this country intervene whenever necessary throughout the world to prevent the subjection of free peoples to Communist-inspired totalitarian regimes at the expense of their national integrity." In an editorial in the *Washington Post*, Sumner Welles warned of the domino effect and declared, "The American people have entered the Valley of Decision," while Lowell Thomas on NBC said Truman's "appeal today was a plea to save the American way." For their part, at least two Republican leaders of Congress also pledged their support in similar terms. Vandenberg, chair of the Senate Foreign Relations Committee, pronounced, "In such a critical moment, the President's hands must be upheld," while Eaton, chair of the House Foreign Affairs Committee, said, "The real issue is whether we are going to stand up and be counted for freedom in the world."[4]

These reactions notwithstanding, though, it would be inaccurate to say that immediate support in the United States was enthusiastic. Rather, there was a sense that Truman had told an unpleasant truth and that Congress and the American people would have to act on it, even if they were not anxious to do so. Radio and newspaper coverage reported that the president "spoke frankly," with "candor," provided a "frank admission," and brought out the issue in "a remarkably forthright way."[5] Yet, media accounts also depicted the "blanched" faces of a "much-shaken Congress" that was "awed," "anxious," and "shocked" although "forewarned" of the content of the speech. Nor were these reactions limited to members of Congress. As *Newsweek* observed, "For the man in the street like the man in Congress, the implications were not comforting."[6]

Some individuals and groups explicitly rejected the president's call. According to Sen. Claude Pepper, aid to Greece and Turkey would "destroy any hope of reconciliation with Russia" and align the United States with "reactionary and corrupt regimes in the world." Henry Wallace's Progressive Citizens of America also denounced Truman's speech, with Wallace arguing that it was nothing more than "a mixture of unsupported assertions, sermonizing and exhortation. It was evident that in the name of crisis facts had been withheld, time had been denied and a feeling of panic had been engendered." On the other end of the political spectrum, Rep. Harold Knutson of Minnesota charged, "I guess the do-gooders won't feel right until they have us all broke."[7]

More often, however, the response was one of anxious, reserved judgment. Senator Taft stated, for instance, "I do not want war with Russia.

Whether our intervention in Greece tends to make such a war more probable or less probable depends on many circumstances regarding which I am not yet fully advised and, therefore, I do not care to make a decision at the present time." Senator Bridges, a vehement anti-Communist, was conflicted and worried that the new policy "knocks budget plans askew." Indeed, when Vandenberg held an off-the-record session with Republican senators, he found that only two were immediately willing to pledge their "all-out support" for Greek-Turkish aid. The others had many questions, such as how the policy would impact the budget and to how many countries the larger policy would apply. Vandenberg encouraged them to submit their questions in writing so that he could get answers. Others had mixed feelings, as well. Eleanor Roosevelt, for example, agreed with the concept of economic aid in her "My Day" column but was distressed that the United States was not going through the United Nations. A majority of American citizens also approved of aid, but surveys showed they nonetheless had concerns about the financial cost of the endeavor, the universality of its application, and the unilateral nature of the administration's proposal. Still, as the *New York Times* discerned, it appeared that a majority in both parties—and, one might add, a majority of the citizenry as a whole—would eventually support the new policy. In words that reflected the rhetorical appeals of realism in Truman's address, Vandenberg implored that it was time to "face facts."[8]

The Critical Nature of Truman's Health in the Ongoing Crisis

While reactions to aid for an ailing Greece rolled in, the president dealt with illness of a more personal sort. A lingering virus, compounded by stress and quite possibly a heart condition, had left Truman utterly exhausted. From Florida, the president wrote to Margaret that he had slept for three hours on the plane to Key West. "No one, not even me (your mother would say I) knew how very tired and worn to a frazzle the Chief Executive had become." In another letter, Truman told Bess, who had remained behind, that he had been too weak to walk to the beach as he usually did and had driven instead. Since his arrival,

Truman admitted, "I have been asleep most of the time." Two days later, the president was feeling better and wrote that his throat was starting to clear. Margaret Truman was to make her singing debut on the radio on Sunday, March 16. Although Truman knew that his wife was as anxious about the event as he was, they agreed that he should remain in Key West to "take some more sun." The vacation, originally scheduled for no more than four days, eventually lengthened into nearly seven.[9]

Truman's appearance and decision to leave for Key West right after his speech proved problematic for the White House. When reporters raised questions about the president's health, Dr. Graham assured them that he simply needed some "sunshine, swimming and relaxation." The physician added that Truman was "in tip-top shape. . . . It's just that he's been going pretty hard lately and he needs a rest." The following day, the *New York Times* reported that Charlie Ross "is still concerned over what he believes are exaggerated pessimistic reports about the President's health." Ross emphasized that Truman was suffering only from mild fatigue and that Dr. Graham had not even accompanied him to Key West, which indicated that no serious illness was involved. Back at the White House, Elsey worried to Clifford that the president's long absence was "bad psychologically" given the persuasive effort underway for Greek-Turkish aid.[10] After declaring Greece to be in a state of crisis, Truman's decision to leave on a week's vacation seemed incongruous.

The president returned to Washington, D.C., on the evening of March 19 but did not appear to feel well. In his diary, Ayers recorded that he met Truman upon his arrival and that the president was "carrying a cane when he got out of the car. In response to my greeting and inquiry as to how he was, he said he was 'all right.' I thought he seemed a little tired and lacking in pep." Ayers surmised that the president's condition was due to the fact that the plane flew at an unusually high altitude to avoid storms, necessitating that those on board use oxygen. A day later on March 20, Ayers recorded that Dr. Graham had alluded, somewhat mysteriously, to the president's health over lunch. He had told Ayers, Ross, White House clerk Maurice Latta, and chair of the Economic Stabilization Administration, Judge Caskie Collett, that

Truman was "not entirely OK. He said he looked well but there was an old condition existing—which he did NOT explain or go into—and which he said he would not want even the President to be told about." According to Graham, the condition could be "controlled" and Truman could be told about it "when he is about to end his term." It is difficult to know what to make of this revelation. Possibly, the White House physician believed the president's state was more serious than he had led Truman to believe; Truman's struggles with lung congestion, in tandem with the difficulty of clearly diagnosing heart problems at the time, may have given the navy doctor's dire prediction more resonance for Graham. If so, however, then why share this information with Latta, Collett, or even Ayers and not, presumably, with others more highly placed within the administration? Graham may have been respond-ing to concerns expressed by Ayers or the others about the president's health, but Ayers did not mention the expression of such worries in his diary. While Graham's conversation with Truman about cardiac asthma clearly indicates that he believed the president suffered from a health condition, his disclosure here appears to have been an effort to impress and/or to reassure his audience. Meanwhile, his puzzling insistence on protecting Truman from such news ensured that the president would not learn that Graham had broken the vow to secrecy he made to Truman in Waco. On March 21, Ayers reported running into Truman and, perhaps prompted by Graham's admission the day before, again inquired how the president felt. Ayers wrote, "he replied, much as he did the other night on his return from Key West, that he felt 'all right.' He gave me the impression, however, that he did not feel too peppy."[11]

Indeed, apprehension over perceptions of the president's health apparently led the White House to launch a low-level counter-cam-paign. On March 24, Dr. Graham met with reporters, telling them that Truman was doing "splendidly" after his vacation. The physician declared that the president "has the constitution of an iron man" and "thrives" on work. When Truman approached the end of his second year in the White House a few weeks later, the administration put forth a major effort. A *New York Times* story quoted Graham as saying that the president had "the energy of the average man twenty years younger." In *Time,* an article gave a complete rundown on a typical busy day for Truman and claimed Graham had deemed him to be "in top condition," adding that Truman's "invariable remark" to Graham was "'You know I don't get sick.'" The *Milwaukee Journal* also ran a story, accompanied by a photo of Truman on a walk, smiling broadly. In an unattributed testimony to Truman's health and "the soundness of his heart," the newspaper pointed to the ease with which he had handled the flight to Mexico when the plane had to fly especially high to avoid bad weather. The newspaper reported, "Several of the older members of the group became very uncomfortable, but the elevation did not bother the president at all."[12] This tale hardly seems believable given Ayers's account of Truman's condition after the high-elevation flight from Key West, particularly since the president's chest congestion on the return from Mexico was what apparently prompted Graham to tell him that he had cardiac asthma. In any event, Truman appeared to have recovered by mid-April, as articles about his health began to dissipate while print coverage on the vitality of Greece and Turkey continued. The president, feeling better, began to participate actively in the public campaign to gain congressional approval for his proposed legislation.

The Continuing Campaign for Greek-Turkish Aid

During Truman's initial absence, however, the administration knew—despite apparent favorable reactions on the part of the public—that it could not afford to be complacent. The administration faced a Republican majority in Congress that was loath to spend money overseas and held but a narrow majority of support among American citizens. As a result, State and the White House engaged in a full-court press from March through May to win public and congressional opinion. Acheson and others appeared at congressional hearings on the proposed aid bill, while the administration made use of other communication resources it had available, as well. On March 15, Henderson and Assistant Secretary of State Willard Thorp appeared on the NBC broadcast, *Our Foreign Policy,* to discuss "Why Are We Helping Greece?," with the State Department releasing transcripts of the recorded program in advance for media use. In early April, Paul A. Porter, back from Greece, would appear on the same program to talk about "What Does the Truman Doctrine Mean?" with Rep. Chester Merrow of New Hampshire, a Republican member of the House Foreign Affairs Committee, who urged support of the administration in order to "stop the spread of totalitarianism" and "help guarantee freedom in this world."[13] Beginning in March and continuing until passage of the Greek-Turkish aid bill in May, the administration blanketed the country with speakers in an effort to reach opinion leaders in business, labor, agriculture, and religion. Treasury Secretary Snyder, Labor Secretary Schwellenbach, Under Secretary of the Navy Sullivan, U.N. Ambassador Warren Austin, and officials from State like Porter, Henderson, and others spoke to a wide variety of audiences.[14] In addition, State kept up its efforts at news management, as Acheson's off-the-record appearance before the American Society of Newspaper Editors suggests. Acheson offered journalists a "synthesis" of history and U.S. foreign relations to help "bring forth the significance of the legislation on aid to Greece and Turkey now pending before the Congress." In mid-April, the president, too, spoke off the record before the same group about the crisis, underscoring the need for assistance and expressing "how much I do appreciate the fact that you have placed this matter before the country in a manner they understood."[15] Truman found other opportunities to reinforce the arguments of this March 12 address in subsequent appearances before the Associated Press and the Association of Radio News Analysts.[16]

During this same time period, the administration and its key Republican ally, Senator Vandenberg, continued the campaign with Congress. Vandenberg and Francis Wilcox, chief of staff of the Senate Foreign Relations Committee, took the questions that senators had submitted, obtained the answers from the executive branch, and created a booklet with all the information, which they then distributed to members of the Senate. When questions arose about Marshall's position on the proposal, he sent a telegram to Vandenberg from Moscow stating,

"I personally, and for the State Department, attach the highest order of urgency to immediate passage of the Greek-Turkish aid legislation." The State Department, in turn, published both the question-and-answer booklet and the telegram as a supplement to its *Bulletin,* along with a letter from Assistant Secretary of State Thorp to Representative Eaton with information that had been requested by the House Foreign Affairs Committee about the cost of foreign aid expenditures. State clearly looked at the *Bulletin* as a tool for both information and persuasion with Congress. Meanwhile, Truman had Sullivan laboring as a liaison between the White House and the Capitol, while supportive Democrats like Alben Barkley worked the Hill and campaigned publicly, as well.[17]

It was Arthur Vandenberg, however, who played the most significant role with Congress. When criticism over bypassing the United Nations began to gain traction, Vandenberg offered his amendment that permitted the United Nations to end U.S. aid if it found that the United Nations could assume responsibility or that aid was no longer needed. Clifford and Acheson seethed over what they perceived as his grandstanding. A few days later, pollster Elmo Roper informed the State Department that adoption of Vandenberg's proposed amendment would move public support from a bare majority to "between two-thirds and three-quarters." Acheson and Truman immediately decided that a copy of Roper's findings should go not only to Barkley on the Senate Foreign Relations Committee but also to Vandenberg.[18] As a result of both the administration's on-going campaign and Vandenberg's leadership, the Senate passed the bill on April 22 with 67 Senators in favor and 23 opposed. The House gave its approval on May 9 by a vote of 287 to 107. On May 22, Truman signed the Greek-Turkish aid bill into law at the Muehlebach Hotel in Kansas City where he was staying while he visited his ill mother in nearby Independence.[19]

Implications of the Truman Doctrine Speech

The Truman Doctrine, as it came to be known, provided assistance to Greece and Turkey that was primarily military in character. In Greece, the aid program included equipment, weapons, American advisors in the field, and, eventually, even napalm and Navy Helldivers. American assistance was an important factor in the Greek government's eventual victory but, as Howard Jones reflected, "American military aid alone had not been solely responsible. The communists could have gone on indefinitely if they had not switched from guerrilla tactics to conventional warfare and if they had continued to receive refuge and outside assistance" from Bulgaria and Yugoslavia. Moreover, military assistance to the Greek government had problematic side effects, for it dampened the Greek government's meager enthusiasm for reforms that might win it popular support. The aid program also forced the U.S. military to grapple with the role of "advisor" versus "combatant," a distinction that could not clearly be made and that would haunt future military advisory ventures in other countries. In Turkey, assistance resulted in the training of thousands of officers and enlisted men and the reorganization of the entire Turkish military so that it was better prepared to resist potential Soviet attacks until U.S. help could arrive. The United States also gained forward bases in Turkey that it could use in the event of a military conflict with the Soviets.[20] In achieving its specific objectives in Greece and Turkey, then, the Truman Doctrine was successful, although its accomplishments in Greece were more ambiguous.

The president's rhetoric also laid the groundwork for the Marshall Plan, which was first aired as a trial balloon in a public affairs outreach speech by Acheson to the Delta Cotton Council in Cleveland, Mississippi, on May 8, 1947, and then developed more fully in Marshall's commencement address at Harvard on June 5, 1947. Even before the president signed the Greek-Turkish aid bill into law, the administration was using its themes to legitimize a massive economic reconstruction program for Europe. The Truman Doctrine and the Marshall Plan were, as Truman later put it, "two halves of the same walnut." The Marshall Plan's focus on economic help diverted attention from the fact that Greek-Turkish aid was mostly military and calmed developing fears that the Truman Doctrine intended, contrary to its claims, to focus on military, rather than economic, assistance to endangered countries.[21] Because of the Marshall Plan, Western European governments were able to allocate immense amounts of money to reconstruction without resorting to austere programs that would have risked social and political unrest. The Truman administration's insistence that these nations cooperate with one another economically and politically—and include Germany, as well—led them, in turn, to require that the United States provide military security through what became the North Atlantic Treaty Organization (NATO). As a result, a longer-term effect of the Truman Doctrine, in conjunction with Soviet efforts to dominate Eastern Europe, was to create two different spheres of influence, definitively dividing Europe for decades to come. The Marshall Plan alarmed the Soviets, who believed it would undermine Soviet influence on Eastern Europe. After threatening Eastern European governments not to participate, the Soviet Union tightened its grip, cracking down on democratization efforts in Hungary and Czechoslovakia, instituting collectivist economic planning, and crushing dissent.[22] The Truman Doctrine helped establish a counterweight to Soviet power, but, by stirring Soviet insecurities, it also inadvertently encouraged the Soviets to solidify their own power base.

Domestically, the Truman Doctrine address also promoted a climate conducive to anti-Communist arguments that would ultimately prove harmful not only to the administration but also to others. The speech's reliance upon the rhetorical stockpile of anti-Communist words and images from the American past made Truman's message compelling in the short term but simultaneously seemed to verify earlier right-wing attacks on the administration, particularly since the president specifically mentioned Yalta.[23] The language of the speech, reinforced in media accounts and perpetuated by others in the public eye, contributed to an atmosphere of fear over danger from both abroad and within. Only two days after Truman's speech, Ayers told reporters that some of the telegrams received at the White House in response to the address were "clearly inspired," while ABC's Martin Agronsky commented that a "prominent and disturbing aftermath of the President's policy declaration is [the] way in which those who criticize it are automatically labeled wild-eyed dreamers, Wallace school liberals or just plain Communists." By early April, the House Un-American Activities Committee was holding hearings on outlawing the Communist Party altogether.[24] The rhetorical stance of realism in Truman's speech suggested that those who disagreed with him were out of touch with reality, while the president's embedded disease metaphors and allusion to "subterfuges" such as "political infiltration" raised the possibility that the United States might fall to Communism through internal means. After all, disease can be deceptive since individuals may appear healthy even though they are infected.[25] Truman appreciated this point all too well, for his own public portrayals of personal health masked chronic underlying issues. Debates about Communism and subversion occurred before the Truman Doctrine speech and would have happened without it, but the president's long silence on the topic of U.S.-Soviet relations ceded, in Medhurst's words, "atmospheric definition and regulation" to Truman's opponents.[26] When the president did speak, his language served to confirm every fear that professional anti-Communists had uttered in the preceding two years, unleashing forces that he could not control, culminating in the bitter attacks that Truman and others suffered from the likes of McCarthy. For example, on March 21, 1947—just nine days after his speech—the president signed into law Executive Order 9835, establishing a government loyalty program, despite the misgivings he had about the FBI's J. Edgar Hoover, whom he loathed, being in charge. The public pressure for a Loyalty Review Board for government employees had been building since 1946, but the themes of Truman's address made it even more difficult for him to counter such pressures or to shape them in ways that would prove less damaging to the careers and reputations of the countless individuals caught in the renewed wave of American anti-Communism.[27]

Internationally, the administration initially applied the Truman Doctrine in a flexible way, but the president eventually found it more difficult to discern when and where national interests demanded U.S. assistance. Truman, in September 1947, explained the practical application of his foreign policy principles. According to the president, "We intend to do our best to provide economic help for those who are prepared to help themselves and each other. But our resources are not unlimited. We must apply them where they can serve the most effectively to bring production, freedom, and confidence back to the world." For these reasons, the administration refused to consider China on a par with Greece and Turkey and, despite enormous pressure to do so, refrained from sending U.S. combat troops to Greece. Slowly but surely, however, the universalistic themes of the Truman Doctrine and the administration's subsequent rhetoric, further energized by the Berlin crisis in 1948 and Mao's victory in 1949, influenced the administration's perceptions of reality. Although the White House was focused on the Soviet Union in 1947, it began to see Communism itself as a larger monolithic threat by 1950, when Truman opined that South Korea was "the Greece of the Far East." He confided to an aide, "If we are tough enough now, there won't be any next step." Korea marked a turning point in the application of American foreign policy, but the Truman Doctrine was the symbolic turning point that made that policy transformation possible. At the same time, Truman's receipt of National Security Council Resolution 68 (NSC 68) just prior to the outbreak of hostilities in Korea encouraged the president eventually to endorse its recommendations for a political, economic, and military buildup, despite his concerns about balancing the budget. The federal government began to divert monies from domestic needs to what President Eisenhower would ominously refer to, in his farewell address, as "the military-industrial complex." While historians Michael Hogan, Arnold Offner, and Raymond Ojserkis rightly noted that it was the Korean War, not NSC 68 in itself, that led the United States to launch the Cold War arms race, the linguistic framework of the Truman Doctrine helped lead the way to Korea.[28]

In the Truman Doctrine speech, the administration had refrained from qualifying which "free peoples . . . resisting attempted subjugation" it would help and had not specifically addressed the Soviet Union as the threat. Rather, the president had relied on extensive fear appeals about totalitarian regimes, specified just once as Communist in nature. These characteristics of the speech, strategically selected for success within the immediate rhetorical situation that the White House faced, had implications that its contributing authors did not foresee. First, the Truman Doctrine's rhetorical framework made it easier for both Truman and his successors to talk about and to perceive the world in bipolar terms.

Beyond Truman's decision to intervene in Korea, later presidents would employ his polarizing themes to heighten the significance of Vietnam. Kennedy wrote in a 1963 magazine article, for example, "Two great forces—the world of communism and the world of free choice—have, in effect, made a 'bet' about the direction in which history is moving." South Vietnam, Laos, and other countries were "points of uncertainty [that] remain," but new nations, too, would have to "choose between two competing systems." In 1966, Johnson likewise would compare the decision to escalate the war in Vietnam with Truman's decision to aid Greece and Turkey.[29] The Truman Doctrine's bipolarity also led the United States to support unsavory governments. Harding Bancroft, an assistant to the U.N. Commission that investigated the Greek crisis in 1947 and a supporter of U.S. intervention, conceded that in Greece, Korea, and elsewhere, "We were forced to back individuals who weren't the greatest of men, as opposed to forms of government, in order to preserve what we regard as democracy as opposed to some form of dictatorship."[30] The Truman Doctrine prompted a trade-off that resulted in resentment from victims of repressive regimes and made the U.S. government vulnerable to charges of hypocrisy. While the Truman Doctrine speech portrayed the world in black-and-white terms, the details of geopolitical struggles more often could be found in shades of gray, a point that the president had but fleetingly acknowledged in his brief admission of the Greek government's imperfection.

Indeed, the Truman Doctrine's depiction of threatening scenes, its promotion of insecurity, and its insistence that the United States must act immediately would recur on a regular basis in the foreign policy rhetoric of the Cold War presidents who followed Truman. The executive branch's use of such discourse also facilitated its gradual assumption of congressional war powers, a point that was not lost on Vandenberg during the campaign for Greek-Turkish aid. As he wrote on March 24, 1947, "The trouble is that these 'crises' never reach Congress until they have developed to the point where Congressional discretion is pathetically restricted. When things finally reach a point where a President asks us to 'declare war' there is usually nothing left except to 'declare war.'"[31] Vandenberg wanted Truman and other presidents to bring issues to the attention of Congress sooner, but he failed to realize what the executive branch had learned: Congress was more willing to defer to presidential wishes when presented with a "crisis" rather than a "troubling issue" or a "problematic state of affairs." The lesson was not lost on future presidents.

In the State Department's extensive news management on behalf of Greek-Turkish aid, one can also see the beginnings of the sophisticated media and public relations operations run by the executive branch today. The State Department's new emphasis upon public affairs in 1947 allowed State to shape news coverage in ways that Charlie Ross and his small operation at the White House could not. In the future, presidents would increasingly attempt to influence the media through a combination of strategy and additional staff. Kennedy, for instance, offered journalists access to his advisors and wooed them with exclusive interviews and not-for-attribution briefings on a much larger scale than previous presidents. With Vietnam, presidents learned how television coverage of war casualties could undermine public support, leading them to even greater efforts at controlling media coverage. The Reagan administration developed the "message of the day," accompanied by pleasing visuals, to entice reporters to cover particular stories from particular perspectives. During the 1984 U.S. invasion of Grenada, the Reagan White House restricted access to combat areas and permitted the release only of approved photos and film, ensuring that one of the first widely distributed visuals was of an American medical student evacuated from the island kissing the ground upon reaching the United States.[32]

Today, the George W. Bush administration offers talking heads for news, opinion, and even entertainment programs; stages events that television, in particular, finds irresistible, such as the toppling of the Saddam Hussein statue in Baghdad; provides exclusive interviews to sympathetic outlets like Fox News; runs a user-friendly website of news and photos (as does the State Department); threatens news organizations that cover stories it deems undesirable; and excludes protesters from presidential appearances through such means as "free speech zones" located far from where the president—and reporters—will be. Too often, the news media have also been accomplices in such efforts; the *New York Times,* ironically, played a major supporting role in the prelude to both Greek-Turkish aid and the second Bush administration's Iraq war.[33] In Truman's day, the State Department had come to realize the importance of winning the public debate. For the contemporary White House, the object has become, sadly, to quash public debate almost entirely.

In the Truman Doctrine speech, one also hears the themes that served to justify later U.S. efforts at championing democracy, efforts that would eventually veer toward imperialism. This is not to say that such ideas were unique to Truman. After all, earlier presidents had used the touchstone of manifest destiny or urged Americans to make the world safe for democracy. The Truman Doctrine speech drew upon this rhetorical history in plotting the United States' more active role in the post–World War II world and gave the pursuit of supporting other free nations added urgency by tying it to U.S. national security. As rhetorical critic Robert Scott observed, it was but a small jump from the containment terminology of the Truman Doctrine to liberation rhetoric, leading many citizens to ask, "If one can justify keeping Greece 'free,' should we not 'free' nations in captivity?" The Eisenhower administration, in fact, embraced liberation arguments publicly to appeal to its core domestic supporters and to citizens in East European nations but privately dismissed a policy of military liberation as too dangerous. Tragically, Hungarians in October 1956 may have taken the administration at its public word, particularly through the liberation arguments that circulated on Radio Free Europe, when they decided to rebel and, receiving no help from the United States, were crushed by Soviet forces.[34]

In the decades that followed, U.S. presidents would regularly justify their military action abroad as necessary to maintain freedom and peace, whether against missiles in Cuba or Communists in Southeast Asia. They also would argue that military action was needed to reinstate democracy in areas where the enemy had recently taken steps to abolish it—as in Grenada and Panama—although they shied away from explicit propositions of liberation for regions long dominated by Communism. Nixon continued to fight against Communists in

Vietnam while, simultaneously, taking steps to establish diplomatic relations with the People's Republic of China. Even Reagan, despite his vehement anti-Communism, engaged in arms talks with the nation he had described as "the evil empire." Although presidents were willing to roll back enemy efforts that upset the balance of power, they refrained—after the experience in Hungary—from advocating liberation that would threaten that balance. Just as Truman declared Communist factions in Greece's civil war were engaged in "terrorist activities," subsequent presidents similarly made use of the terrorist terminology. For example, Kennedy and Johnson attacked Communist "terrorists" in Vietnam. By the time of the buildup to the 1991 Persian Gulf War, Pres. George H. W. Bush was arguing that the United States must take action against Iraq not only to defend peace and freedom (and to restore the government of Kuwait) but also to create "a new era, freer from the threat of terror, stronger in the pursuit of justice, and more secure in the quest for peace."[35]

Presidents after Truman justified interventions—often following his lead in sidestepping the United Nations and acting unilaterally—as a means to contain the enemy or to restore democracy where the enemy had recently abolished it; however, George W. Bush's rhetoric about the war on terror and the war in Iraq went one step further to advocate the establishment of democracy around the globe. In Bush's words, one also hears echoes of the Truman Doctrine speech in, for instance, the president's insistence that "Either you are with us, or you are with the terrorists," a line that recalls Truman's division of the world into "alternative ways of life." Bush's public messages have served to reenergize the Cold War dualism of freedom versus Communism and to transform it into freedom versus terrorism.[36] In his rhetoric, the president has linked the war against terrorism with the war in Iraq by equating both with the struggle against totalitarianism on behalf of democracy. Where presidents after Eisenhower were more circumspect about arguing for liberation, Bush's rhetoric and the policies deriving from that rhetoric have boldly called for democratization. As the president told troops at Fort Bragg in July 2006, "By achieving victory in Iraq, we will help Iraqis build a free nation in the heart of a troubled region, and inspire those who desire liberty—those democratic reformers from Damascus to Tehran." Iraq, Bush maintained, was just one battle point in the war on terror, "a global struggle against the followers of a murderous ideology that despises freedom and crushes all dissent, and has territorial ambitions and pursues totalitarian aims."[37] The president has also compared the fight against terrorism with the Cold War fight against Communism. According to Bush, "Like the ideology of communism, our new enemy is dismissive of free peoples." However, he maintained, "It is courage that keeps an untiring vigil against the enemies of a rising democracy. And it is courage in the cause of freedom that once again will destroy the enemies of freedom."[38] The president has even gone so far as to make explicit comparisons between his foreign policy and that of Truman, while members of his administration have compared Bush to Truman himself.[39]

Perhaps it is not surprising, then, that on July 25, 2006, Greek demonstrators protesting U.S. involvement in Iraq and Israeli attacks on Lebanon knocked over the statue of Harry Truman in Athens that had been erected there in 1963 by the American Hellenic Educational Progressive Association in honor of his Greek-Turkish policy.[40] In part, the response was a reaction to the immediate policies of the United States and its closest Middle East ally. The act also may have been tinged with anti-Semitism, particularly given Truman's recognition of Israel. In another sense, however, there was an implicit link between Truman and the current U.S. administration, for President Truman's words gave voice to a doctrine that rhetorically shaped subsequent presidential messages and policies. This is not to lay blame for Bush White House policies at Truman's feet, for he likely would have been horrified at the thought that the United States would impose its way of life on others. Yet, words often have implications that those who formulate and use them do not foresee.

Final Thoughts

Viewed from the vantage point of rhetorical and political history, the Truman Doctrine speech must be judged unwise. It helped the White

House gain congressional assent to aid for Greece and Turkey and laid the groundwork for the Marshall Plan, but the address and accompanying campaign also had many long-term, negative consequences. As John Lewis Gaddis has pointed out, some form of Cold War clash was inevitable, given Stalin's complete control over the Soviet government and his raging insecurities.[41] Nevertheless, Truman's speech and corresponding policies clearly stoked those insecurities and simultaneously heightened American fears, as well. The terminological framework of the Truman Doctrine gradually came to dominate American worldviews, while Soviet responses—both instigated by Stalin and by the Truman Doctrine's aggravation of Stalin—served to fortify the framework's perceived reality. Had Truman chosen to speak earlier about the potential conflict, he could have exerted greater control over the form that conflict would take. Instead, the president's long silence, followed by the sudden and frightening turnaround of the Truman Doctrine speech, reinforced the exaggerated claims of right-wing critics and fairly soon stiffened Stalin's resolve, as well. Truman's rhetoric in March 1947 would contribute to the unfettered anti-Communism of McCarthyism, to the eventual application of the Truman Doctrine in a universalistic way, and to the expenditure of lives and dollars on a staggering scale as the United States committed itself to places like Korea and Vietnam and to winning the arms race. Moreover, the Truman Doctrine speech provided themes that future U.S. presidents would use to justify military interventions—often unilateral in nature—and the assumption of ever-greater executive powers, all in the service of democracy. The State Department's news management efforts likewise set an example for future administrations that is perhaps nowhere clearer than in George W. Bush's campaign to go to war in Iraq and American journalism's extensive complicity in this endeavor. While Harry Truman is not responsible for the sins of those who followed him, the inescapable legacy of the Truman Doctrine address cannot be ignored. In the rhetoric of the war on terror, the reverberations of the Truman Doctrine speech continue to be felt.

NOTES

Special Message to the Congress on Greece and Turkey

1. Harry S. Truman, Special Message to the Congress on Greece and Turkey: The Truman Doctrine, Mar. 12, 1947, Public Papers of the Presidents 1947 (Washington, D.C.: United States Government Printing Office, 1963), 176–80.

Chapter 1. Prelude to Cold War Crisis

1. Clifford, *Counsel to the President*, 134; Jones, Suggestions, "Drafts of Truman Doctrine [Folder I]," Jones Papers, Personal Papers and Organizational Records, Truman Library (hereafter cited as PPOR); Jones, *Fifteen Weeks*, 17; "Truman Routine," *New York Times*, Feb. 22, 1947, A3.

2. For example: James Reston, "Truman Asks," *New York Times*, Feb. 28, 1947, A1; Dept. of State News Digest, Feb. 28, 1947, "Dept. of State-News Digests-Jan. 2–Mar. 4, 1947 [Folder 1]," Staff Member and Office Files (hereafter cited as SMOF): Conway Files—Subject File, Truman Papers.

3. Ernest K. Lindley, "Significance," *Newsweek*, Mar. 10, 1947, 24; Radio Comment of March 7, "Summaries of Radio Comment and Newspaper Editorials—Mar. 1947" folder, SMOF: Conway Files—Subject File, Truman Papers; Hanson Baldwin, "World Role," *New York Times*, Mar. 2, 1947, A4.

4. "Let the People," *Washington Daily News*, Mar. 10, 1947, A24, in "Foreign Relations-Truman Doctrine [1 of 3]," Elsey Papers: Truman Presidency Subject File, PPOR.

5. Entry for Mar. 12, 1947, Ayers Diary, "Jan. 1, 1947–June 30, 1947," Ayers Papers, PPOR; Margaret Truman, *Souvenir*, 160–62.

6. Jones, *Fifteen Weeks,* 17–18; C. P. Trussell, "Congress," *New York Times,* Mar. 13, 1947, A4.

7. "Let the Nations," *Newsweek,* Mar. 24, 1947, 24; Trussell, "Congress," A4.

8. "Truman, Ill," *New York Times,* Feb. 1, 1947, A7; entry for Mar. 7, Harry S. Truman 1947 Diary; Truman to Margaret Truman, Mar. 13, 1947, in Margaret Truman, *Harry S. Truman,* 343; Truman to Bess Truman, Mar. 15, 1947, in Ferrell, ed., *Dear Bess,* 544.

9. "Let the Nations," *Newsweek,* Mar. 24, 1947, 24; Special Message to Congress, Mar. 12, 1947, www.americanrhetoric.com; "President's Delivery," *Washington Post,* Mar. 13, 1947, in "Foreign Relations-Truman Doctrine [1 of 3]" folder, Elsey Papers: Truman Presidency Subject File, PPOR.

10. "Crisis," *Compact Edition of Oxford English Dictionary.*

11. See Bostdorff, *Presidency and Rhetoric of Foreign Crisis.*

12. Zarefsky, "Rhetorical Cold War."

13. Hinds and Windt, *Cold War as Rhetoric,* 5.

14. Medhurst, "Introduction," 7.

15. Aristotle, *Rhetoric,* Book I: 1355b. Also see: Medhurst, "Rhetoric and Cold War," 19–27.

16. Elsey, "Impressions of a Speechwriter," 55.

17. Elsey, Oral History, July 10, 1969, 163, Truman Library.

18. See, for example: Ferrell, *American Diplomacy,* 255; Entry for Feb. 1, "American Economic Mission to Greece '47, Diary 2-'47" folder, Porter Papers, PPOR; Constantine Tsaldaris, Oral History, May 4, 1964, 12–13, Truman Library.

Chapter 2. Turning Points, 1945–47

1. Hamby, "Harry S. Truman," 15–20; Pierce, Woodrow Wilson and Harry Truman, 162–66; Medhurst, "Truman's Rhetorical Reticence," 52–53, 61–64.

2. Medhurst, "Truman's Rhetorical Reticence," 53–60.

3. Crockatt, *Fifty Year War,* 52–54.

4. Truman, Address on Foreign Policy, Oct. 27, 1945, *Public Papers of the President* (hereafter cited as *PPP*), 434, 435; Byrnes quoted in Hinds and Windt, *Cold War as Rhetoric,* 72–73.

5. Hinds and Windt, *Cold War as Rhetoric,* 75–77; Stalin, "Analysis of Victory," 2: 142, 143, 144–47.

6. Larson, *Origins of Containment*, 253–54; Hinds and Windt, *Cold War as Rhetoric*, 77; Truman quoted in Costigliola, "Creation of Memory and Myth," 46.

7. Forrestal, *Forrestal Diaries*, 134; Costigliola, "Creation of Memory and Myth," 38; Harbutt, *Iron Curtain*, 156.

8. Stalin, "Analysis of Victory," 2: 146; Hinds and Windt, *Cold War as Rhetoric*, 77; Ulam, *Rivals*, 108; Costigliola, "Creation of Memory and Myth," 45; Larson, *Origins of Containment*, 255.

9. Kennan, *Memoirs*, 192–93.

10. Hinds and Windt, *Cold War as Rhetoric*, 70–72.

11. Kennan, Long Telegram, Feb. 22, 1946, in "Correspondence Files—USSR, 1945–1946," Roberts Papers, PPOR.

12. Ibid.

13. Ibid. Also see: Hinds and Windt, *Cold War as Rhetoric*, 80; Chilton, *Security Metaphors*, 145–47; Ivie, "Realism Masking Fear," 70; Kennan, *Memoirs*, 294.

14. Byrnes quoted in Larson, *Origins of Containment*, 256, and Mathews and Henderson quoted in De Santis, *Diplomacy of Silence*, 175; Acheson, *Present at the Creation*, 151. Also see: Chilton, *Security Metaphors*, 137; Miscamble, *George F. Kennan*, 26–27.

15. Kennan, *Memoirs*, 295.

16. Elsey, *Unplanned Life*, 137–38.

17. Vandenberg, *Private Papers*, 246–49.

18. Gaddis, *United States*, 305, 306; Byrnes, *All in One Lifetime*, 349–50; also see: Robertson, *Sly and Able*, 486–87.

19. Vaughn, Oral History, Jan. 16, 1963, 137–39, Truman Library.

20. Churchill, "Sinews of Peace," 5. See Hinds and Windt, *Cold War as Rhetoric*, 90–91, and Chilton, *Security Metaphors*, 163–64, on the origins of "iron curtain."

21. Churchill, "Sinews of Peace," 6–7.

22. Anderson, *United States, Great Britain*, 112–15.

23. Byrnes, *All in One Lifetime*, 349; Truman, News Conference, Mar. 8, 1946, *PPP*, 145; Harbutt, *Iron Curtain*, 161; Ferrell, *Harry S. Truman*, 234–35; Anderson, *United States, Great Britain*, 115–16; Elsey, *Unplanned Life*, 137.

24. Hinds and Windt, *Cold War as Rhetoric*, 98–99; Ferrell, *Harry S. Truman*, 235.

25. McFarland, "Iranian Crisis," 241–45; Kuniholm, *Origins of the Cold War*, 205, 274–75.

26. McFarland, "Iranian Crisis," 245–47; Kuniholm, *Origins of the Cold War,* 192–98.

27. McFarland, "Iranian Crisis," 250–52; Robertson, *Sly and Able,* 471; Truman quoted in Hamby, *Man of the People,* 349; Ayers, in Ferrell, *Truman in the White House,* 139; Truman, News Conference, Mar. 8, 1946, *PPP,* 146.

28. Byrnes quoted in Robertson, *Sly and Able,* 472–73, also see 474.

29. Gaddis, *United States,* 336–37; Anderson, *United States, Great Britain,* 136; Truman, *Memoirs,* 1: 375–77, and 2: 96–97; Acheson, *Present at the Creation,* 195–96; Woods and Jones, *Dawning of the Cold War,* 235–36.

30. Byrnes quoted in Robertson, *Sly and Able,* 479.

31. Wallace quoted in Culver and Hyde, *American Dreamer,* 419; Truman Diary Entry of Sept. 17, 1946, quoted in Ferrell, ed., *Off the Record,* 94.

32. Truman, News Conference, Sept. 12, 1946, *PPP,* 426–27, 428.

33. Clifford, *Counsel to the President,* 118.

34. Hinds and Windt, *Cold War as Rhetoric,* 116; Wallace, "Way to Peace," 104, 103; White and Maze, *Henry A. Wallace,* 228. Quotations from Wallace's speech are taken from Walton who reproduced Wallace's reading copy from the Henry Wallace Papers at the University of Iowa as the most reliable version available. See: Wallace, "Way to Peace," 100–108.

35. Wallace, "Way to Peace," 103–104; Walton, *Henry Wallace,* 109.

36. Schapsmeier and Schapsmeier, *Prophet in Politics,* 155; Culver and Hyde, *American Dreamer,* 422; Vandenberg, *Private Papers,* 301.

37. Footnote to Truman, News Conference, Sept. 12, 1946, *PPP,* 427; Clifford, *Counsel to the President,* 119.

38. Wallace quoted in Culver and Hyde, *American Dreamer,* 423; Byrnes, *All in One Lifetime,* 354, 373–76; Robertson, *Sly and Able,* 479.

39. Culver and Hyde, *American Dreamer,* 423; Margaret Truman, *Harry S. Truman,* 317.

40. Truman, News Conference, Sept. 20, 1946, *PPP,* 431.

41. Wallace quoted in White and Maze, *Henry A. Wallace,* 232.

42. Ibid., 237.

43. Underhill, *Truman Persuasions,* 192–93; Clifford to Truman, Sept. 24, 1946, "Report by Clark Clifford, 'American Relations with the Soviet Union,'" SMOF: Conway Files—Subject Files, Truman Papers; Elsey, *Unplanned Life,* 142.

44. Clifford, *Counsel to the President,* 125; Hinds and Windt, *Cold War as Rheto-*

ric, 119; *American Relations with the Soviet Union*, Sept. 24, 1946, "Report by Clark Clifford, 'American Relations with the Soviet Union.'"

45. *American Relations with the Soviet Union.*

46. Ibid.

47. Clifford, *Counsel to the President*, 123–24; Krock, *Memoirs*, 419–82. In correspondence with the author (Apr. 7, 2006), Elsey noted that the version Clifford shared with Krock was a copy of the "last typed version" prior to the final bound one.

48. Elsey, Correspondence with Author, Apr. 7, 2006; Clifford to Truman, Sept. 24, 1946, "Report by Clark Clifford, 'American Relations with the Soviet Union'"; Clifford, Oral History, Apr. 13, 1971, 70, Truman Library; Clifford, Oral History, Apr. 19, 1971, 152, Truman Library; Clifford, *Counsel to the President*, 115, 125; Elsey, *Unplanned Life*, 142–43.

49. Clifford to Truman, Sept. 24, 1946, "Report by Clark Clifford, 'American Relations with the Soviet Union.'"

50. Woods and Jones, *Dawning of the Cold War*, 136; Elsey, *Unplanned Life*, 143; Truman quoted in Ferrell, *Harry S. Truman*, 249.

51. Ferrell, *Harry S. Truman*, 227; Forrestal, *Forrestal Diaries*, 102; Ferrell, "Diplomacy," 41–42, 45–48; Painter, *Cold War*, 5; Paterson, *Meeting the Communist Threat*, 45–46; Marshall quoted in Stoler, *George C. Marshall*, 161.

52. Ferrell, *Harry S. Truman*, 228–30; Hamby, *Man of the People*, 379–81; Truman, Radio Report to the Nation Announcing the Lifting of Major Price Controls, Oct. 14, 1946, *PPP*, 451–55.

53. Acheson, *Present at the Creation*, 200.

54. Leffler, *Preponderance of Power*, 141, "'International' Budget," *New York Times*, Feb. 5, 1947, A22.

55. McCullough, *Truman*, 180–81; Hamby, *Man of the People*, 211–12; Ferrell, *Harry S. Truman*, 165–67, 218, 180; Margaret Truman, *Bess W. Truman*, 218.

56. Graham, Oral History, Mar. 30, 1989, online, Truman Library; Hamby, *Man of the People*, 487; Harry Truman to Bess Truman, Nov. 18, 1946, in Ferrell, ed., *Dear Bess*, 540.

57. Kuniholm, *Origins of the Cold War*, 401; Bevin quoted by Tsaldaris, Oral History, May 4, 1964, 3–4; Acheson, *Present at the Creation*, 199; Mark Ethridge, Oral History, Jan. 1976, 31, Truman Library.

58. Byrnes to Truman, July 4, 1945, and Truman to Acheson, Dec. 22, 1945, both

in "Greece," President's Secretary's Files (hereafter cited as PSF): Subject File, 1945–53, Truman Papers; Anderson, *United States, Great Britain*, 146–47; President's Calendar, Dec. 20, 1946, based on Matthew J. Connelly Files, www.trumanlibrary .org/calendar, Truman Library; Memorandum of Conversation by the Secretary of State [Byrnes], Jan. 4, 1947, *Foreign Relations of the United States* (hereafter cited as *FRUS*), 1.

59. Kuniholm, *Origins of the Cold War*, 86–90; also see: Gerolymatos, *Red Acropolis*, 55, 72–82, 158–60.

60. *Intelligence Review*, No. 50, Jan. 30, 1947, "Jan. 1947 [Nos. 46–50]," SMOF: Naval Aide to the President Files, Truman Papers; Marshall to Embassy in Greece, Jan. 21, 1947, *FRUS*, 10.

61. A. N. Overby to Snyder, Dec. 20, 1946, "Greece—General, 1946–1949," Snyder Papers, PPOR; Entry for Feb. 1, 1947, Porter Diary, "American Economic Mission to Greece '47, Diary 2 '47," Porter Papers.

62. Gerolymatos, *Red Acropolis*, 113; Close, *Origins of the Greek Civil War*, 137–41; De Santis, *Diplomacy of Silence*, 123–25; Bohlen, *Witness to History*, 161–64; Overby to Snyder, Dec. 20, 1946, "Greece—General, 1946–1949," Snyder Papers; Halifax quoted in Anderson, *United States, Great Britain*, 165.

63. Anderson, *United States, Great Britain*, 163–64; Ambassador to Turkey (Edwin Wilson) to Byrnes, Jan. 17, 1947, *FRUS*, 7; Porter quoted in Anderson, *United States, Great Britain*, 164.

64. Anderson, *United States, Great Britain*, 165–68; Kuniholm, *Origins of the Cold War*, 406–407.

65. Marshall quoted in Stoler, *George C. Marshall*, 159; Henderson, Oral History, June 14, 1973, 76, Truman Library; British Embassy to Dept. of State, *Aide-Memoires*, Feb. 21, 1947, *FRUS*, 32–37; Acheson, *Present at the Creation*, 217.

66. MacVeagh to Marshall, Feb. 7, 1947, 15–16; MacVeagh to Marshall, Feb. 11, 1947, 17; Porter to William Clayton, Under Secretary for Economic Affairs, Feb. 17, 1947, 17–22. All in *FRUS*.

67. Ethridge to Marshall, Feb. 17, 1947, *FRUS*, 24–25; Marshall to Embassy in Greece, Feb. 18, 1947, *FRUS*, 25.

68. Gallman to Marshall, Feb. 19, 1947, 26–27; Memorandum of Conversation by Henderson of Meeting with Marshall, Henderson, Lord Inverchapel, and Herbert Sichel, First Secretary of the British Embassy, Feb. 24, 1947, 43–44; Ambassador to the Soviet Union (Walter Bedell Smith) to Byrnes, Jan. 8, 1947, 2–3. All in *FRUS*.

69. Clifford, *Counsel to the President*, 131–32; Truman, *Memoirs*, 2: 99.

70. Acheson, *Present at the Creation*, 213.

71. Ibid., 131, 119; Porter to Cohen, Feb. 19, 1947, *FRUS*, 26, and footnote on 26; MacVeagh to Marshall, Feb. 20, 1947, *FRUS*, 28.

72. Kuniholm, *Origins of the Cold War*, 240–44, 407–09; Acheson to Marshall, "Crisis and Imminent Possibility of Collapse in Greece," Feb. 21, 1947, *FRUS*, 29–31; MacVeagh to Marshall, Feb. 18, 1947, *FRUS*, 28.

73. Acheson to Marshall, "Crisis," 29–31; Acheson, *Present at the Creation*, 217; Pogue, *George C. Marshall*, 162 and footnote on 561.

74. Ethridge to Marshall, Feb. 21, 1947, *FRUS*, 37–39.

75. Henderson, Oral History, 78–84; "Memorandum Regarding Proposals Contained in British *Aide-Memoires* of February 21 Relating to Greece and Turkey," Transmitted to Marshall, Feb. 24, 1947, *FRUS*, 41–42. Also see: Memorandum by the Chairman of the Special Committee to Study Assistance to Greece and Turkey (Henderson) to the Under Secretary of State (Acheson), undated but submitted to Marshall on Feb. 26, 1947, *FRUS*, 47–48, with attachments of "Analysis of the Proposals Contained in British Notes of February 24 Relating to Greece and Turkey (For Discussion Purposes Only)," 48–52, and "Positions and Recommendations of the Department of State Regarding Immediate and Substantial Aid to Greece and Turkey," *FRUS*, 52–55; Jones, *Fifteen Weeks*, 132–33; Acheson, *Present at the Creation*, 218.

76. Henderson, Oral History, 80; Acheson, *Present at the Creation*, 218.

77. Marshall to Embassy in Greece, Feb. 18, 1947, *FRUS*, 25. For Marshall on Communism in Greece, see: Marshall to Embassy in Greece, Feb. 17, 1947, *FRUS*, 22–23.

78. For additional information on Great Britain's efforts in this regard, see Anderson, *United States, Great Britain*, 20–21. For more on the relationship of Tito and Stalin with the Greek Communists, see Banac, "Tito-Stalin Split," 258–73, and Gerolymatos, *Red Acropolis*, 124–25. May, *"Lessons" of the Past*, 44–45, sheds light on what the Truman administration chose to pay attention to and what it ignored, while Conway, "Greek Civil War," 28–29, examines how Soviet archives later revealed that Stalin, in 1945–47, was "not quite the ruthless opportunist" that he would become after the Marshall Plan.

79. Medhurst, "Truman's Rhetorical Reticence," 59; Dirksen, "Red Fascism," 359; "Soviets Held Peril by Styles Bridges," *New York Times*, Feb. 1, 1947, A4; Hinds and Windt, *Cold War as Rhetoric*, 31–60.

80. Truman to Eleanor Roosevelt, May 7, 1947, "Correspondence of Harry S. Truman and Mrs. Franklin D. Roosevelt, 1945–1957," Eleanor Roosevelt Papers, Franklin D. Roosevelt Library, on microfilm at Truman Library, PPOR.

81. Clifford, *Counsel to the President*, 131; Acheson, *Present at the Creation*, 218; Acheson, Interview, "Memoirs—Acheson, Dean, Feb. 18, 1955, A.M." Post-Presidential *Memoirs* Interviews with Associates, Post-Presidential Papers, Truman Library; Jones, *Fifteen Weeks*, 129, 134.

82. President's Daily Appointments, Feb. 18, 1947, "February 1947 Daily Sheets," PSF: President's Appointments File—Daily Sheets File, Truman Papers; Marshall quoted in Bland and Bland, *George C. Marshall*, 331.

Chapter 3. The Campaign Begins

1. Elsey Notes, Mar. 9, 1947, "1947, Mar. 12, Truman Doctrine," Elsey Papers: Speech File.

2. "Analysis of the Proposals Contained in British Notes" and "Positions and Recommendations of the Department of State," both attached to Memorandum by the Chairman of the Special Committee to Study Assistance to Greece and Turkey (Henderson) to the Under Secretary of State (Acheson), undated but submitted to Marshall on Feb. 26, 1947, all in *FRUS*, 47–55; Henderson, Oral History, 82–83.

3. President's Calendar, Feb. 24, 1947; Acheson, *Present at the Creation*, 218–19; Forrestal, *Forrestal Diaries*, 245–46.

4. Stuart, *Department of State*, 391, 400–405; Russell, Oral History, July 13, 1973, online, Truman Library.

5. Stuart, *Department of State*, 403–405, 426–27; Russell, Oral History.

6. Russell, Oral History; Stuart, *Department of State*, 427–28; Dept. of State Press Release, Mar. 14, 1947, Transcript of *Our Foreign Policy*, "Miscellaneous Mimeo Speeches," Jones Papers.

7. Russell, Oral History.

8. Jones, *Fifteen Weeks*, 135, 150.

9. Stuart, *Department of State*, 384, 413, 426, 436.

10. Jones, *Fifteen Weeks*, 11–12.

11. Acheson, *Present at the Creation*, 219; Jones, *Fifteen Weeks*, 137–38; Truman, *Memoirs*, 2: 100; "Positions and Recommendations," *FRUS*, 53; Memorandum by

Secretaries of State, War, and the Navy, attached to Memorandum by Marshall to Truman, Feb. 26, 1947, *FRUS*, 59–60.

12. Acheson, *Present at the Creation*, 219.

13. Ibid.; Jones, *Fifteen Weeks*, 139–42; also see: Jones, Notes on Acheson's Presentation to Department Working Group, Feb. 28, 1947, "Drafts of Truman Doctrine [Folder I]," Jones Papers.

14. Jones, *Fifteen Weeks*, 141; Truman, *Memoirs*, 2: 103–104; Vandenberg, *Private Papers*, 338–39; Lyle Wilson, "Greek Crisis," *Washington Daily News*, Mar. 12, 1947, in "Foreign Relations—Truman Doctrine (Clippings)," Elsey Papers: Harry S. Truman Administration Subject File; Statement by Marshall, undated, submitted to Truman on Feb. 27, 1947, *FRUS*, 60–62.

15. Statement by Marshall, 60–62; Acheson, Interview, "Memoirs—Acheson, Dean, Feb. 18, 1955, A.M.," Post-Presidential *Memoirs* Interviews with Associates.

16. For more on the metaphors used, see: Chilton, *Security Metaphors*, 197–98; Hinds and Windt, *Cold War as Rhetoric*, 138–39; Ivie, "Fire, Flood," 571–75.

17. Jones, "The Drafting of the President's Message to Congress on the Greek Situation," Mar. 12, 1947, and "The Drafting of the President's Message of March 12, 1947," both in "Drafts of Truman Doctrine [Folder I]," Jones Papers; Jones, *Fifteen Weeks*, 143.

18. Vandenberg, *Private Papers*, 339; Truman, *Memoirs*, 2: 103–104; Acheson, *Present at the Creation*, 219; Goldman, *Crucial Decade*, 59; Acheson to Robert Patterson, Mar. 5, 1947, *FRUS*, 94; Acheson to Marshall, Mar. 7, 1947, *FRUS*, 97.

19. Ross's Press and Radio Conference, Feb. 27, 1947, "Press & Radio Conferences, Feb. 3–Mar. 31, 1947," Ross Papers: Papers Removed from Scrapbooks, PPOR; Report on the Meeting of the State-War-Navy Coordinating Committee (SWNCC) Subcommittee on Foreign Policy Information, Feb. 28, 1947, *FRUS*, footnote 2 on 67; Dept. of State News Digest, Feb. 28, 1947, "Dept. of State—News Digests—Jan. 2–Mar. 4, 1947 [Folder 1]," in SMOF: Conway Files—Subject File; Chomsky, "Advance Agent"; Reston, "Truman Asks," A1.

20. Acheson, *Present at the Creation*, 220; Jones, "The Drafting of the President's Message to Congress on the Greek Situation."

21. Jones, *Fifteen Weeks*, 150–51; Jones, "The Drafting of the President's Message of March 12, 1947"; Russell, "Memorandum on Genesis of Truman's March 12 Speech," Mar. 17, 1947, *FRUS*, 121–23; Russell, Oral History.

22. Jones, Notes on Acheson's Presentation to Dept. Working Group.

23. SWNCC Subcommittee on Foreign Policy Information, "Informational Objectives and Main Themes," undated but approved Mar. 3, 1947, *FRUS*, 76–78.

24. Jones, *Fifteen Weeks*, 152, 144.

25. Lindley, "Significance," *Newsweek*, Mar. 10, 1947, 24; Newspapers Quoted in Dept. of State News Digest, Mar. 7, 1947, "Dept. of State—News Digests—Mar. 5–May 28, 1947 [Folder 2]," SMOF: Conway Files—Subject File; "U.S. Faces," *Life*, Mar. 17, 1947, 31; Anne O'Hare McCormick, "Unfinished," *New York Times*, Mar. 5, 1947, A24; "Policy," *Newsweek*, Mar. 10, 1947, 23; Radio Comment of Mar. 4 and Mar. 5, 1947, both in "Summaries of Radio Comment and Newspaper Editorials—Mar. 1947," SMOF: Conway Files—Subject File.

26. "Policy," *Newsweek*, Mar. 17, 1947, 27; Baldwin, "World Role," *New York Times*, Mar. 2, 1947, A4.

27. Bertram Hulen, "U.S. Note," *New York Times*, Mar. 2, 1947, A1; Radio Comment of Mar. 3, 1947, "Summaries of Radio Comment and Newspaper Editorials—Mar. 1947," SMOF: Conway Files—Subject File; "War on Chaos," *New York Times*, Mar. 2, 1947, B10.

28. Poulos, "Report," Filed Mar. 9, *New Republic*, Mar. 17, 1947, 26–27.

29. Engel and Taft quoted in Hulen, "U.S. Note," A1, A4.

30. Parry-Giles, *Rhetorical Presidency*, 4, 6–7; Chomsky, "Advance Agent." In fairness, it should be noted that Poulos was a former OWI employee, too, so such an affiliation did not automatically lead to favorable coverage for the government.

31. Chomsky, "Advance Agent"; Jones, *Fifteen Weeks*, 169.

32. Jones, *Fifteen Weeks*, 145.

33. Text of the statement is included in Marshall to Embassy in Greece, Mar. 4, 1947, *FRUS*, 87.

34. "Policy," *Newsweek*, Mar. 17, 1947, 27; "U.S. Faces," *Life*, Mar. 17, 1947, 31; Bertram Hulen, "Greek Aid," *New York Times*, Mar. 5, 1947, A1; "Containing Operation," *New Republic*, Mar. 17, 1947, 5; Wilson, "Greek Crisis," *Washington Daily News*, Mar. 12, 1947, in "Foreign Relations—Truman Doctrine (Clippings)," Elsey Papers: Harry S. Truman Administration Subject File. For use of "containment," see: C. L. Sulzberger, "Urgency," *New York Times*, Mar. 5, 1947, A18; UP Ticker Highlights, Dept. of State News Digest, Mar. 5, 1947, "Dept. of State—News Digests—Mar. 5, 1947–May 28, 1947," SMOF: Conway Files—Subject File; "Policy," *Newsweek*, Mar. 17, 1947, 27; "Containing," *New Republic*, Mar. 17, 1947, 6.

35. Clifford, *Counsel to the President*, 134; "President: Viva," *Newsweek*, Mar. 17, 1947, 28; Entry for Mar. 7, 1947, Harry S. Truman 1947 Diary. Although Truman's diary gives the date of March 7, the Daily Presidential Appointments Diary reveals that he was in Waco on March 6.

36. Huget, "Secret Heart of Harry Truman"; Medline Plus Medical Dictionary; Sopko quoted in Huget, "Secret Heart of Harry Truman"; Entry for May 31, 1947, Ayers Diary, "Jan. 1, 1947–June 30, 1947," Ayers Papers; Graham, Oral History.

37. Shafer, interview with author, June 23, 2006; Margaret Truman, *Bess W. Truman*, 166–67; Graham, Oral History.

38. Shafer, interview with author, July 14, 2006; "Rays Purify," *New York Times*, Dec. 28, 1947, A14.

39. West, *Upstairs at the White House*, 64.

40. "Truman 'Like a Man,'" *New York Times*, Mar. 4, 1947, A3.

41. Entry for Mar. 1, 1947, Ayers Diary, "Jan. 1, 1947–June 30, 1947," Ayers Papers; Truman, Address on Foreign Economic Policy, Mar. 6, 1947, *PPP*, 167–68.

42. Initial Press and Radio Reaction to the President's Speech on U.S. Foreign Economic Policy—Waco, Texas, Mar. 6, 1947, "January–March 1947," PSF: Speech File—Speeches: Drafts & Press Releases.

43. Ibid.; Editorial Reactions to Current Events: President's Speech at Waco, Texas, Mar. 14, 1947, "January–March 1947," PSF: Speech File—Speeches: Drafts & Press Releases.

44. Memorandum to Marshall from Acheson, Mar. 7, 1947, *FRUS*, 99; Acheson, *Present at the Creation*, 221; Clifford, *Counsel to the President*, 142; Notes on Cabinet Meeting, Mar. 7, 1947, "Notes on Cabinet Meetings—Post-Presidential File (Set I) Jan. 3–Dec. 19, 1947," Connelly Papers, PPOR.

45. Cabinet Meeting, Mar. 7, 1947, "Notes on Cabinet Meetings—Post-Presidential File (Set I) Jan. 3–Dec. 19, 1947," Connelly Papers; Forrestal, *Forrestal Diaries*, 252; Ross's Press and Radio Conference, Mar. 7, 1947, "Press & Radio Confs. Feb. 3–Mar. 31, 1947," Ross Papers: Papers Removed from Scrapbooks.

46. Entry for Mar. 3–Mar. 6, 1947, Ayers Diary, "Jan. 1, 1947–June 30, 1947," Ayers Papers; James Reston, "Direct Approach," *New York Times*, Mar. 7, 1947, A8; Initial Press and Radio Reaction to the President's Speech on U.S. Foreign Economic Policy—Waco, Texas, Mar. 6, 1947.

47. Entry for Mar. 10, 1947, Ayers Diary, "Jan. 1, 1947–June 30, 1947," Ayers Papers; Harold B. Hinton, "Truman Postpones," *New York Times*, Mar. 8, 1947, A4.

48. Acheson, *Present at the Creation*, 221; Truman, *Memoirs*, 2: 105.

49. Harold B. Hinton, "President to Ask," *New York Times*, Mar. 11, 1947, A1.

50. Jones, *Fifteen Weeks*, 163.

Chapter 4. Opportunity through Threat

1. George, *Managing U.S.-Soviet Rivalry*, 1; Memo, Elsey to Clifford, Mar. 7, 1947, "1947, Mar. 12, Speech to Congress [re aid to Greece and Turkey]," Clifford Papers: Presidential Speech File, PPOR.

2. Kennan, *Memoirs*, 319–20; Jones, *Fifteen Weeks*, 154–55; Bohlen, *Witness to History*, 261.

3. Elsey, interview with author, June 23, 2005.

4. "The World," *Time*, Mar. 24, 1947, 18–20; "Behind Truman's," *Newsweek*, Mar. 24, 1947, 15; Untitled Clipping, *New York Tribune*, Mar. 13, 1947, in "Foreign Relations—Truman Doctrine [1 of 3]," Elsey Papers: Truman Presidency Subject File; Jones, *Fifteen Weeks*, 148; Acheson, *Present at the Creation*, 220–21.

5. Elsey, Oral History, Apr. 9, 1970, 297–98, Truman Library; Elsey, "Truman Doctrine," 4; Clifford, Oral History, Apr. 19, 1971, 151, 145–51; Clifford, *Counsel to the President*, 133–37.

6. Truman, *Memoirs*, 2: 105; Clifford, *Counsel to the President*, footnote on 136; Elsey, "Truman Doctrine," 4.

7. Carlin, "Harry S. Truman," 40, 53; Underhill, *Truman Persuasions*, 207; Clifford, Oral History, Apr. 19, 1971, 150.

8. "Positions and Recommendations," *FRUS*, 53–54; Acheson, *Present at the Creation*, 218–19; Jones, *Fifteen Weeks*, 136–37; Henderson, Oral History, 100; Acheson, Oral History, Feb. 18, 1955, 35, Truman Library.

9. Jones, "Chronology" and "The Drafting of the President's Message to Congress," both in "Drafts of the Truman Doctrine [Folder I]," Jones Papers; Jones, *Fifteen Weeks*, 150–52.

10. Jones, "The Drafting of the President's Message to Congress"; Jones, *Fifteen Weeks*, 153. Also: Jones, "Suggestions for the President's Message to Congress in Regard to the Greek Situation," Mar. 2–3, 1947; Henderson, Draft of Truman Doctrine Speech; and Merriam, Draft of Truman Doctrine Speech: all three items in "Drafts of Truman Doctrine [Folder I]," Jones Papers.

11. Jones, March 4 Draft Corrected by Jones Prior to Official March 4 Draft,

Mar. 4, 1947, "Drafts of Truman Doctrine [Folder I]," Jones Papers; Jones, *Fifteen Weeks*, 153–54; Jones, "Chronology"; Jones, "The Drafting of the President's Message to Congress"; Merriam, Draft of Truman Doctrine Speech; Background Memorandum on Greece, Mar. 3, 1947, "The Truman Doctrine: Folder 1," www.trumanlibrary.org/whistlestop/study_collections; Acheson's Annotated Copy of Jones' Official Draft of Mar. 4 and Henderson, Draft of the Truman Doctrine Speech, "Drafts of the Truman Doctrine [Folder I]," Jones Papers; Request from Paul Economou-Gouras to Marshall, Mar. 3, 1947, "Drafts of the Truman Doctrine [Folder I]," Jones Papers; Jones, President's Message to Congress on Greek Situation, Official Draft of Mar. 4, 1947, "Drafts of the Truman Doctrine [Folder I]," Jones Papers.

12. Jones, "The Drafting of the President's Message to Congress"; Jones, *Fifteen Weeks*, 152–53; Russell, "Basic United States Policy" in SWNCC Subcommittee on Foreign Policy Information, "Informational Objectives and Main Themes," undated but approved Mar. 3, 1947, *FRUS*, 76–78; Jones' Annotated Copy of Official Draft of Mar. 4 and Acheson's Annotated Copy of Jones' Official Draft of Mar. 4, both in "Drafts of Truman Doctrine [Folder I]," Jones Papers; Henderson, Draft of Truman Doctrine Speech.

13. Jones, "Chronology"; Jones, "The Drafting of the President's Message to Congress"; Jones, *Fifteen Weeks*, 153–54.

14. Jones, "Chronology"; Jones, "The Drafting of the President's Message to Congress"; Jones, *Fifteen Weeks*, 154; Acheson's Annotated Copy of Jones' Official Draft of Mar. 4.

15. Jones, *Fifteen Weeks*, 159; Jones' Annotated Copy of Official Draft of Mar. 4; Jones, Mar. 6 Draft, "Drafts of Truman Doctrine [Folder I]," Jones Papers; Jones, "Chronology." Acheson does not discuss the meeting between Jones and him in his memoirs, nor his reflections on what FDR would have done, probably out of deference to Truman, for whom he came to have a great deal of respect and affection.

16. Acheson, *Present at the Creation*, 221; Clifford, *Counsel to the President*, footnote on 142; Jones, "Chronology" and *Fifteen Weeks*, 167.

17. Cable from Marshall to Acheson, Mar. 7, 1947, *FRUS*, 100–101.

18. Elsey, "Truman Doctrine," 1; Clifford, *Counsel to the President*, 133–34; Jones, "Chronology" and "The Drafting of the President's Message to Congress."

19. Jones, "Chronology" and "The Drafting of the President's Message to

Congress"; Clifford, *Counsel to the President*, 134–35; Elsey, "Truman Doctrine," 4; Jones' Annotated Copy of Mar. 7 Draft and Notes, "Drafts of the Truman Doctrine [Folder I]," Jones Papers.

20. Jones, "Chronology" and *Fifteen Weeks*, 153–54; Jones' Annotated Copy of Mar. 7 Draft; Jones' Annotated Copy of Mar. 9 Draft, "Drafts of the Truman Doctrine [Folder I]," Jones Papers.

21. Clifford, *Counsel to the President*, 135; Elsey, "Truman Doctrine," 4; Elsey's Annotated Copy of Mar. 9 Revision and Elsey's Annotated Copy of Mar. 9 Draft, Both in "Foreign Relations—Truman Doctrine [2 of 3] [2001 accretion]," Elsey Papers: Truman Presidency Subject File; Clifford's Annotated Copy of Mar. 9 Draft, "1947, Mar. 12, Speech to Congress [re aid to Greece and Turkey]," Clifford Papers: Presidential Speech File; Elsey, Oral History, July 10, 1969, 168–69; Elsey, interview with author.

22. Elsey, "Truman Doctrine," 4; Elsey's Annotated Copy of Mar. 9 Revision; Elsey's Annotated Copy of Mar. 10 Draft, "Foreign Relations—Truman Doctrine [2 of 3] [2001 accretion]," Elsey Papers: Truman Presidency Subject File; Clifford, *Counsel to the President*, 136.

23. Memo from Marx Leva for John Sullivan to Forrestal, Mar. 8, 1947, "1947, Mar. 12, Speech to Congress [re: aid to Greece and Turkey]," Clifford Papers: Presidential Speech File; Clifford, *Counsel to the President*, 137; Elsey's Annotated Copy of Mar. 9 Draft; Clifford's Annotated Copy of Mar. 9 Draft; Elsey's Annotated Copy of Mar. 9 Revision; Jones, "The Drafting of the President's Message to Congress," "Chronology," and *Fifteen Weeks*, 157. In the March 7 Cabinet meeting, Leahy expressed similar views on the relevance of capitalism when he said, "The people of the U.S. should be brought in and told—it is Communism or free enterprise." See: Notes of Cabinet Meeting, Mar. 7, 1947.

24. Elsey's Annotated Copy of Mar. 9 Draft; Clifford's Annotated Copy of Mar. 9 Draft; Elsey's Annotated Copy of Mar. 10 Draft; Elsey's Annotated Copy of Mar. 9 Revision; Elsey, "Truman Doctrine," 4; Elsey, Oral History, Apr. 9, 1970, 358–59; Russell, Oral History; Jones *Fifteen Weeks*, 159–60; Notes by Elsey, Apr. 3, 1947, "1947, April 5 Jefferson Day Speech," Elsey Papers: Speech File.

25. Clifford's Annotated Copy of Mar. 9 Draft; Elsey's Annotated Copy of Mar. 9 Draft; Elsey's Annotated Copy of Mar. 10 Draft; Draft of Mar. 10, 1947, "1947, Mar. 12, Truman Doctrine," Elsey Papers: Speech File; Jones, *Fifteen Weeks*, 156; Jones' Annotated Copy of Mar. 7 Draft; Elsey's Annotated Copy of Mar. 9 Revision; Clifford, *Counsel to the President*, 135.

26. Elsey's Annotated Copy of Mar. 9 Revision; Elsey's Annotated Copy of Mar. 10 Draft.

27. Clifford, *Counsel to the President*, 137; Elsey, "Truman Doctrine," 4; Elsey's Annotated Copy of Mar. 10 Draft; Carlin, "Harry S. Truman," 61; Elsey, interview with author.

28. Clifford, Oral History, July 26, 1971, 297, Truman Library; Elsey, interview with author; Elsey's Annotated Copy of Mar. 10 Draft.

29. Truman's Annotated Copy of Mar. 10 Draft, "Speeches—Longhand Notes, Jan.–Mar. 1947," PSF: Speech File. Elsey (in interview with author) believes that Truman's ghostwriters for his memoirs relied upon an Arthur Krock column that erroneously gave Truman credit for changing "shall" to "must." See Arthur Krock, "'Must' Is the Key Word," *New York Times*, Mar. 24, 1947, E3.

30. Elsey's Annotated Copy of Mar. 10 Draft; also see Jones' Annotated Copy of Mar. 10 Draft, "Drafts of Truman Doctrine [Folder 2]," Jones Papers.

31. Clifford, Oral History, Apr. 19, 1971, 151, 149; also Elsey's Annotated Copy of Mar. 10 Draft and Jones' Annotated Copy of Mar. 10 Draft.

32. Truman's Annotated Copy of Mar. 11 Draft, "Speeches—Longhand Notes, Jan.–Mar. 1947," PSF: Speech File; Elsey's Annotated Copy of Mar. 11 Draft and also the Final Draft of Mar. 11, both in "Foreign Relations—Truman Doctrine [2 of 3] [2001 accretion]," Elsey Papers: Truman Presidency Subject File; Elsey, interview with author; Elsey, Oral History, July 10, 1969, 169.

33. Elsey Notation on Final Draft of Mar. 11; Clifford's Annotated Delivery Copy of Final Draft of Mar. 11, "1947, Mar. 12, Speech to Congress [re aid to Greece and Turkey]," Clifford Papers: Presidential Speech File; Reading Copy of Message to Congress re: Greece and Turkey, Mar. 12, 1947, "Jan.–Mar. 1947; 1945–1953 Presidential Speeches—Originals," PSF: Speech File; White and Henderlider, "What Harry Truman Told Us," 41.

34. Clifford, *Counsel to the President*, 134.

35. Truman on Cicero quoted in White and Henderlider, "What Harry Truman Told Us," 39.

36. Underhill, *Truman Persuasions*, 184. Also see: Ryan, *Harry S. Truman*, 25, and Brockriede and Scott, *Moments in the Rhetoric*, footnote 14 on page 17 on method of residues as the form of refutation that Truman used.

37. Humelsine to Elsey, Mar. 10, 1947, "Foreign Relations—Truman Doctrine [2 of 3] [2001 accretion]," Elsey Papers: Truman Presidency Subject File; Vandenberg, *Private Papers*, 346.

38. Aristotle, *Rhetoric*, Book I: 1355a.

39. Kuniholm, *Origins of the Cold War*, 27–72; Jones, *Fifteen Weeks*, 155; Minutes of Meeting of the Secretaries of State, War, and Navy, Mar. 12, 1947, *FRUS*, 109.

40. Jones, *Fifteen Weeks*, 162–63.

41. Wilson, "Address to Congress," 42.

42. Jones, Notes on Acheson's Presentation to Working Group; McKellar and Acheson quoted in "Russia Protests," *New York Times*, Feb. 16, 1947, A1; Molotov quoted in "U.S. Note," *New York Times*, Feb. 19, 1947, A1; Entry for May 22–23, 1947, Ayers Diary, "Jan. 1, 1947–June 30, 1947," Ayers Papers.

43. κρ'ισις, *Liddell and Scott's Greek-English Lexicon*.

44. Halle, *Cold War as History*, 121.

45. Lanham, *Handlist of Rhetorical Terms*, 11.

46. For example, see: Walton, *Henry Wallace*, 144; Halle, *Cold War as History*, 121.

47. Clifford, *Counsel to the President*, 139–40; Acheson, *Present at the Creation*, 225; Elsey, interview with author.

48. Leva for Sullivan to Forrestal, Mar. 8, 1947, "1947, Mar. 12, Speech to Congress [re aid to Greece and Turkey]," Clifford Papers: Presidential Speech File.

49. Howard Jones, "Reassessment of the Truman Doctrine," 26.

50. Ibid., 31; Woods and Jones, *Dawning of the Cold War*, 245–46.

51. *Public Attitudes toward American Foreign Policy*, May 1947, "Public Attitudes toward American Foreign Policy [1 of 2]," Office of Government Reports, SMOF: Jackson Files.

52. Memorandum on Cost of War, "1947 [2 of 12, Feb.]," Elsey Papers: Chronological File.

53. McMahon, "'By Helping Others,'" 234–36; also see: Bostdorff and Goldzwig, "Idealism and Pragmatism."

54. Lakoff and Johnson, *Metaphors We Live By*, 3, 15; Gregg, "Embodied Meaning," 61; Beer and De Landtsheer, "Metaphors, Politics," 13.

55. Ivie, "Fire, Flood," 571.

56. Chilton, "Meaning of Security," 197–98; also see: Chilton, *Security Metaphors*. For more on the treatment of freedom as fragile in American foreign policy argument, see: Ivie, "Ideology of Freedom."

57. For more, see: Gregg, "Kenneth Burke's Prolegomena."

58. Underhill, *Truman Persuasions,* 9, 338; Hart, *Verbal Style,* 72–73; McKerrow, "Truman and Korea," 5; Elsey, Oral History, July 10, 1969, 170–71.

59. Also see: Ivie, "Fire, Flood," 581. For Ivie's analysis of how Truman's plain style interacted with symbols of savagery in his Korean War rhetoric, see: Ivie, "Literalizing."

60. Beer and Hariman, "Realism and Rhetoric," 6, 3–4.

Chapter 5. Reflections on the Truman Doctrine Speech

1. "Let the Nations," *Newsweek,* Mar. 24, 1947, 24; Jones, *Fifteen Weeks,* 23.

2. "Let the Nations," *Newsweek,* Mar. 24, 1947, 24; Truman quoted in Margaret Truman, *Harry S. Truman,* 343.

3. Dept. of State Foreign Press Summary, Mar. 25, 1947, "Dept. of State—Foreign Press Summaries, Mar. 10, 1946–April 16, 1947," SMOF: Conway Files—Subject File; Churchill quoted in "New World," *Time,* Mar. 24, 1947, 25; *Intelligence Review,* No. 57, Mar. 20, 1947, 22, in "March 1947 [Nos. 55–58]," SMOF: Naval Aide to the President Files—War Dept. Intelligence Review File.

4. See: Telegrams in "PPF 200—Message to Congress on Aid to Turkey and Greece 3/12/47 [Pro]," PPF: Speeches, and "PPF 200—Message to Congress 3/12/47 [Con]," President's Personal File (PPF): Speeches. Also see: Entry for Mar. 13, 1947, Ayers Diary, "Jan. 1, 1947–June 30, 1947," Ayers Papers; Editorial Reaction, "Greece," in PSF: Subject File, 1945–53; Felix Belair Jr., "Truman Acts," *New York Times,* Mar. 13, 1947, A1; Sumner Welles, "Valley of Decision," *Washington Post,* Mar. 13, 1947, in "Foreign Relations—Truman Doctrine [1 of 3]," Elsey Papers: Truman Presidency Subject File; Radio Comment of Mar. 12, "Summaries of Radio Comment and Newspaper Editorials—Mar. 1947," SMOF: Conway Files—Subject File; Robert C. Albright, "Truman Asks," *Washington Post,* Mar. 13, 1947, in "Foreign Relations—Truman Doctrine [1 of 3]," Elsey Papers: Truman Presidency Subject File.

5. See: *Kansas City Times,* Mar. 13, 1947, "Jan.–Mar. 1947," in Summaries of Newspaper Reactions, PSF: Speech File; Radio Comment of Mar. 12 and Mar. 13, in "Summaries of Radio Comment and Newspaper Editorials—Mar. 1947," SMOF: Conway Files—Subject File.

6. Trussell, "Congress," A1, A4; Albright, "Truman Asks"; Dept. of State News Digest, Mar. 13, 1947, "Dept. of State News Digests, Mar. 5–May 28, 1947 [Folder 2]," in SMOF: Conway Files; "America's Date," *Newsweek,* Mar. 24, 1947, 23.

7. Pepper quoted in Hartmann, *Truman and the 80th Congress*, 63; "PCA Denounces," *New York Times*, Mar. 13, 1947, A3; Henry Wallace, "The State Department's Case," *New Republic*, Apr. 7, 1947, 12; Knutson quoted in "America's Date," *Newsweek*, Mar. 24, 1947, 23.

8. Drew Pearson, "The Washington Merry-Go-Round," clipping, Mar. 19, 1947, and Eleanor Roosevelt, "I Cannot Accept Parts of President Truman's Speech," My Day Column, *Washington Daily News* clipping, Mar. 15, 1947, both in "Foreign Relations—Truman Doctrine [1 of 3]," Elsey Papers: Truman Presidency Subject File; Bridges quoted in "America's Date," *Newsweek*, Mar. 24, 1947, 23; Elmo Roper, *Public Opinion Survey of Reactions to President Truman's Proposal Regarding Greece and Turkey*, "State Dept. File: Correspondence, 1946–47 [3 of 5]," White House Central Files (hereafter cited as WHCF): Confidential Files; George Gallup, "Truman's Greek Policy Winning Wide Public Support," Press Release, Mar. 28, 1947, "Public Opinion News Service Release, 1947," American Institute of Public Opinion Records, PPOR; Belair, "Truman Acts"; Vandenberg quoted in Dept. of State News Digest, Mar. 13, 1947, "Dept of State News Digests, Mar. 5–May 28, 1947 [Folder 2]," SMOF: Conway Files.

9. Truman quoted in: Margaret Truman, *Harry S. Truman*, 343; Margaret Truman, *Bess W. Truman*, 304; Ferrell, ed., *Dear Bess*, 544. Also see: Ross's Press and Radio Conference, Mar. 12, 1947, in "Press & Radio Confs. Feb. 3–Mar. 31, 1947," Ross Papers: Papers Removed from the Scrapbooks; Entry for Mar. 19, 1947, Appointments Diary, "Appointments Diary 1947 [2 of 8]," SMOF: Connelly Files.

10. Harold B. Hinton, "President Starts," *New York Times*, Mar. 13, 1947, A1; "Keyed Up," *Newsweek*, Mar. 24, 1947, 24; Hinton, "Players," A5; Notes by Elsey, Mar. 20, 1947, "1947 [3 of 12]," Elsey Papers: Chronological File.

11. Entries for Mar. 19, Mar. 20, and Mar. 21, 1947, Ayers Diary, "Jan. 1, 1947–June 30, 1947," Ayers Papers.

12. "Truman an 'Iron Man,'" *New York Times*, Mar. 24, 1947, A16; "After Two Years," *Time*, Apr. 7, 1947, 23; "Nearly 63," *Milwaukee Journal*, Apr. 19471,3, A1, A3, clipping in "General," PSF: Political File.

13. State Dept. Press Release, Mar. 14, 1947, "Miscellaneous Mimeo Speeches," Jones Papers; Transcript of *Our Foreign Policy*, Apr. 5, 1947, "Speeches and Articles, 1945–76 [Folder 3]," Porter Papers: Personal File.

14. Snyder, Oral Histories, Oct. 30, 1968, 1098–99, and Feb. 26, 1969, 1165–67, Truman Library. For examples of such campaign work, see: W. W. Schroeder of

National Bank of Commerce in New Orleans to Snyder, Apr. 19, 1947, "Speech-Correspondence File 1947 [Folder 4]," Snyder Papers: Speech-Correspondence File; Labor Dept. Press Release of Address by Secretary Schwellenbach before Commonwealth Club in San Francisco, Mar. 20, 1947, "Foreign Affairs & Economic Assistance—Greece & Turkey," SMOF: Clifford Files; Text of Address by John L. Sullivan before Naval Industrial Association, Apr. 9, 1947, "Statements & Addresses: July 2, 1945–Dec. 20, 1947," Sullivan Papers: Statements and Addresses, PPOR; Text of Address by Warren Austin to U.S. Associates of International Chamber of Commerce, May 6, 1947, "Foreign Relations: Speeches & Statements," Elsey Papers: Subject File; State Dept. Press Release of Address by Henry Villard to Annual District Conference of 194th Rotary District at Charlotte, N.C., May 5, 1947, "Foreign Affairs & Economic Assistance—Greece & Turkey," SMOF: Clifford Files; Text of Speech by Loy Henderson before Chicago Council on Foreign Relations, Apr. 14, 1947, "Foreign Affairs & Economic Assistance—Greece & Turkey," SMOF: Clifford Files; Text of Speech by Paul A. Porter before Chicago Council on Foreign Relations, May 9, 1947, "Speeches and Articles, 1945–76 [Folder 3]," Porter Papers: Personal Files.

15. Acheson, Text of Address Made off the Record before the American Society of Newspaper Editors, Apr. 18, 1947, "Speeches & Articles, 1936–1971: American Society of Newspaper Editors—April 18, 1947," Acheson Papers: Publications File, PPOR; Truman, Remarks at a Meeting with the American Society of Newspaper Editors, Apr. 17, 1947, *PPP*, 208, 210.

16. Truman, Address in New York City at the Annual Luncheon of the Associated Press, Apr. 21, 1947, *PPP*, 211–16; The President's Special Conference with the Association of Radio News Analysts, May 13, 1947, *PPP*, 238–41.

17. Wilcox, Oral History, Feb. 10, 1984, 60; "Aid to Greece and Turkey," Supplement to the Dept. of State *Bulletin*, May 4, 1947, "Greece—General," Howard Papers: General File, PPOR; Sullivan, Oral History, Mar. 27, 1972, 31–32, Truman Library; "Barkley Defends," *New York Times*, May 11, 1947, A26.

18. Notes by Elsey, Apr. 3, 1947, "1947, April 5 Jefferson Day Speech," Elsey Papers: Speech File. Also: Roper, *Public Opinion Survey*, and John R. Steelman to Acheson, Apr. 16, 1947, both in "State Dept. File: Correspondence, 1946–47 [3 of 5]," WHCF: Confidential Files.

19. Hartmann, *Truman and the 80th Congress*, 63–64; also see folder, "Missouri, Grandview: April–May 1947," PSF: Trip File, 1945–53.

20. Howard Jones, "Reassessment of the Truman Doctrine," 31, 34; Woods and Jones, *Dawning of the Cold War,* 245–46; Painter, *Cold War,* 19.

21. Truman quoted in Ferrell, *Harry S. Truman,* 257; see Jones, *Fifteen Days,* 208, about these concerns.

22. Painter, *Cold War,* 21–22; Gaddis, *We Now Know,* 50.

23. Medhurst, "Truman's Rhetorical Reticence," 66.

24. Entry for Mar. 14, 1947, Ayers Diary, "January 1, 1947–June 30, 1947," Ayers Papers; Radio Comment of Mar. 17, "Summaries of Radio Comment and Newspaper Editorials—Mar. 1947," SMOF: Conway Files—Subject File; "Communists: Outlaw or Curb?," *Time,* Apr. 7, 1947, 25.

25. For more, see: Shimko, "Power of Metaphors," 209, and Gregg, "Embodied Meaning," 67.

26. Medhurst, "Truman's Rhetorical Reticence," 52.

27. Executive Order 9835 reprinted in Bernstein and Matusow, *Truman Administration,* 358–63. For Truman's views on Hoover and the loyalty program, see Elsey, *Unplanned Life,* 146.

28. Truman, Address before the Rio de Janeiro Inter-American Conference for the Maintenance of Continual Peace and Security, Sept. 2, 1947, *PPP,* 429; Howard Jones, "Reassessment of the Truman Doctrine," 25; Gaddis, "Was the Truman Doctrine," 393–94; Kuniholm, *Origins of the Cold War,* 419; Newman, "NSC (National Insecurity) 68," 55–94; Dwight Eisenhower, Farewell Address, Jan. 17, 1961, *PPP,* 1035–40; Offner, *Another Such Victory,* 422, 470; Hogan, *Cross of Iron,* 304–305; Ojserkis, *Beginnings of the Cold War,* 79–106.

29. John Kennedy, Magazine Article, "Where We Stand," Jan. 15, 1963, *PPP,* 20; Lyndon Johnson, Remarks at a Democratic Party Dinner in Chicago, May 17, 1966, *PPP,* 518.

30. Bancroft, Oral History, June 25, 1974, online, Truman Library.

31. See Bostdorff, *Presidency and the Rhetoric of Foreign Crisis;* Vandenberg, *Private Papers,* 342–43.

32. Bostdorff, *Presidency and the Rhetoric of Foreign Crisis,* 34, 184, 234–37; Thompson, *Ten Presidents,* 70; Krock, "Mr. Kennedy's Management," 82, 199.

33. For more on U.S. news coverage leading up to the 2003 start of the Iraq war, see Massing, "Now They Tell Us," 1, 3.

34. Scott, "Cold War Rhetoric," 10; Tudda, "Reenacting the Story," 3–4, 32–33.

35. Bostdorff, *Presidency and the Rhetoric of Foreign Crisis,* 208–10; George H. W.

Bush, Nationwide Address, Aug. 8, 1990, *Weekly Compilation of Presidential Documents*, 1216–18; Winkler, *In the Name of Terrorism*, 17–28; George H. W. Bush, Iraqi Aggression in the Persian Gulf, Sept. 11, 1990, online.

36. George W. Bush, Address before a Joint Session, Sept. 20, 2001, *Weekly Compilation of Presidential Documents*, 1349; Bostdorff, "George W. Bush," 303–305.

37. George W. Bush, Fourth of July Address to Troops at Fort Bragg, N.C., July 4, 2006, online.

38. George W. Bush, Speech on War on Terror at National Endowment for Democracy, Oct. 6, 2005, online.

39. George W. Bush, State of the Union, Jan. 31, 2006, and Commencement Address at the United States Military Academy at West Point, May 27, 2006, both online; Remarks in Charlotte, N.C., Apr. 6, 2006, online; Miles, "Rumsfeld Cites Truman," online. For more on U.S. presidents and rhetoric dealing with democratization, see Ivie, *Democracy*.

40. Reuters News Service, "Greek Protesters," online.

41. Gaddis, *We Now Know*, 292–94.

BIBLIOGRAPHY

Harry S. Truman Presidential Library

HARRY S. TRUMAN PAPERS
Post-Presidential Papers
Post-Presidential *Memoirs* Interviews with Associates
Presidential Papers
President Harry S. Truman's 1947 Diary, www.trumanlibrary.org/
diary/transcript.
President's Calendar, based on Matthew J. Connelly Files, www.
trumanlibrary.org/calendar.
President's Personal File (PPF): Speeches.
President's Secretary's Files (PSF): Political File; President's Appoint-
ments File; Speech File; Subject File; Trip File.
Staff Member and Office Files (SMOF): Clark M. Clifford Files; Mat-
thew J. Connelly Files; Rose Conway Files; Charles W. Jackson Files;
Naval Aide to the President Files.
White House Central Files (WHCF): Confidential Files

MOTION PICTURE COLLECTION

ORAL HISTORIES: Dean Acheson: February 18, 1955; Harding F. Ban-
croft: June 25, 1974, www.trumanlibrary.org/oralhist/bancroft.html;
Clark M. Clifford: April 13, 1971, April 19, 1971, July 26, 1971; George
M. Elsey: July 10, 1969, April 9, 1970; Mark Ethridge: January 1976; Dr.

Wallace Graham: March 30, 1989, www.trumanlibrary.org/oralhistory/ grahamw.htm; Loy W. Henderson: June 14, 1973; Francis Russell: July 13, 1973, www.trumanlibrary.org/oralhistory/russellf.htm; John W. Snyder: October 30, 1968, February 26, 1969; John L. Sullivan: March 27, 1972; Constantine Tsaldaris: May 4, 1964; Gen. Harry H. Vaughn: January 16, 1963; Francis O. Wilcox: February 10, 1984.

PERSONAL PAPERS AND ORGANIZATIONAL RECORDS (PPOR): Dean Acheson Papers; American Institute of Public Opinion Records; Eben A. Ayers Papers; Clark M. Clifford Papers; Matthew J. Connelly Papers; George M. Elsey Papers; Harry N. Howard Papers; Joseph M. Jones Papers; Paul A. Porter papers; Frank N. Roberts Papers; Eleanor Roosevelt Papers (on microform at the Truman Library, courtesy of the Franklin D. Roosevelt Library); Charles G. Ross Papers; John W. Snyder Papers; John L. Sullivan Papers.

THE TRUMAN DOCTRINE; PROJECT WHISTLESTOP. www.trumanlibrary. org/whistlestop/study_collections.

Secondary Sources

Acheson, Dean. *Present at the Creation: My Years in the State Department.* New York: W. W. Norton, 1969.

Anderson, Terry H. *The United States, Great Britain, and the Cold War, 1944–1947.* Columbia: University of Missouri Press, 1981.

Aristotle. *The Rhetoric.* Translated by W. Rhys Roberts. New York: Modern Library, 1954.

Banac, Ivo. "The Tito-Stalin Split and the Greek Civil War." In *Greece at the Crossroads: The Civil War and Its Legacy.* Edited by John O. Iatrides and Linda Wrigley, 258–73. University Park: Pennsylvania State University Press, 1995.

Beer, Francis A., and Christ'l De Landtsheer. "Metaphors, Politics, and World Politics." In *Metaphorical World Politics.* Edited by Francis A. Beer and Christ'l De Landtsheer, 5–52. East Lansing: Michigan State University Press, 2004.

Beer, Francis A., and Robert Hariman. "Realism and Rhetoric in International Relations." *Post-Realism: The Rhetorical Turn in International Relations.* Edited by Francis A. Beer and Robert Hariman, 1–30. East Lansing: Michigan State University Press, 1996.

Bernstein, Barton J., and Allen J. Matusow, eds. *The Truman Administration: A Documentary History.* New York and London: Harper & Row, 1966.

Bland, Larry I., and Joellen K. Bland, eds. *George C. Marshall: Interviews and Reminiscences for Forrest C. Pogue.* 1986. Rev. ed., Lexington, Va.: George C. Marshall Research Foundation, 1991.

Bohlen, Charles E. *Witness to History, 1929–1969.* New York: W. W. Norton, 1973.

Bostdorff, Denise M. "George W. Bush's Post–September 11 Rhetoric of Covenant Renewal: Upholding the Faith of the Greatest Generation." *Quarterly Journal of Speech* 89 (2003): 293–319.

———. *The Presidency and the Rhetoric of Foreign Crisis.* Columbia: University of South Carolina Press, 1994.

Bostdorff, Denise M., and Steven R. Goldzwig. "Idealism and Pragmatism in American Foreign Policy Rhetoric: The Case of John F. Kennedy and Vietnam." *Presidential Studies Quarterly* 24 (1994): 515–30.

Brockriede, Wayne, and Robert L. Scott. *Moments in the Rhetoric of the Cold War.* New York: Random House, 1970.

Byrnes, James F. *All in One Lifetime.* New York: Harper and Brothers, 1958.

Bush, George W. Commencement Address at the United States Military Academy at West Point. May 27, 2006. www.whitehouse.gov

———. Fourth of July Speech to Troops at Fort Bragg, N.C. July 4, 2006. www.presidentialrhetoric.com.

———. Remarks in Charlotte, N.C. April 6, 2006. Federal News Service. LexisNexis.

———. Speech on War on Terror at National Endowment for Democracy. October 6, 2005. www.whitehouse.gov.

———. State of the Union. January 31, 2006. www.whitehouse.gov

Bush, George H. W. Iraqi Aggression in the Persian Gulf. September 11, 1990. www.presidentialrhetoric.com.

Carlin, Diana B. "Harry S. Truman: From Whistle-Stops to the Halls of Congress." In *Presidential Speechwriting: From the New Deal to the Reagan Revolution and Beyond.* Edited by Kurt Ritter and Martin J. Medhurst, 40–67. College Station: Texas A&M University Press, 2003.

Chilton, Paul A. "The Meaning of Security." In *Post-Realism: The Rhetorical Turn in International Relations.* Edited by Francis A. Beer and Robert Harriman, 193–216. East Lansing: Michigan State University Press, 1996.

———. *Security Metaphors: Cold War Discourse from Containment to Common House.* New York: Peter Lang, 1996.

Chomsky, Daniel. "Advance Agent of the Truman Doctrine: The United States, *The New York Times,* and the Greek Civil War." *Political Communication* 17 (October–December 2000). Accessed through EBSCOhost.

Churchill, Winston. "Sinews of Peace." March 5, 1946. Westminster College. Fulton, Mo. Available at the Churchill Centre. www.winstonchurchill.org

Clifford, Clark, with Richard Holbrooke. *Counsel to the President.* New York: Random House, 1991.

Close, David. *The Origins of the Greek Civil War.* New York and London: Longman, 1995.

The Compact Edition of the Oxford English Dictionary. 2d ed. New York: Oxford University Press, 1994.

Conway, Martin. "The Greek Civil War: Greek Exceptionalism or Mirror of a European Civil War?" In *The Greek Civil War: Essays on a Conflict of Exceptionalism and Silences.* Edited by Philip Carabott and Thanasis D. Sfikas, 17–39. Burlington, Vt.: Ashgate, 2004.

Costigliola, Frank. "The Creation of Memory and Myth: Stalin's 1946 Election Speech and the Soviet Threat." In *Critical Reflections on the Cold War: Linking Rhetoric and History.* Edited by Martin J. Medhurst and H. W. Brands, 38–54. College Station: Texas A&M University Press, 2000.

Crockatt, Richard. *The Fifty Year War: The United States and the Soviet Union in World Politics, 1941–1991.* London and New York: Routledge, 1995.

Culver, John C., and John Hyde. *American Dreamer: A Life of Henry A. Wallace.* New York: W. W. Norton, 2000.

De Santis, Hugh. *The Diplomacy of Silence: The American Foreign Service, the Soviet Union, and the Cold War, 1933–1947.* Chicago: University of Chicago Press, 1980.

Dirksen, Everett. "Red Fascism." January 23, 1947. *Vital Speeches of the Day* 13 (April 1, 1947): 358–62.

Elsey, George M. Correspondence with Author. April 7, 2006.

———. "Impressions of a Speech Writer." In *The Truman Doctrine of Aid to Greece: A Fifty-Year Retrospective.* Edited by Eugene T. Rossides, 55–59. Washington, D.C., and New York: Academy of Political Science and American Hellenic Institute Foundation, 1998.

———. Interview with Author. Washington, D.C. June 23, 2005.

———. "The Truman Doctrine: The Speech." *Whistle Stop,* The Harry S. Truman Library Institute Newsletter 25, no. 3 (1997): 1, 4.

———. *An Unplanned Life.* Columbia: University of Missouri Press, 2005.

Ferrell, Robert H. *American Diplomacy: The Twentieth Century.* 4th ed. New York: W. W. Norton, 1988.

———, ed. *Dear Bess: The Letters from Harry to Bess Truman, 1910–1959.* New York: W. W. Norton, 1983.

———. "Diplomacy without Armaments, 1945–1950." In *The Romance of History.* Edited by Scott L. Bills and E. Timothy Smith, 35–49. Kent, Ohio: Kent State University Press, 1997.

———. *Harry S. Truman: A Life.* Columbia and London: University of Missouri Press, 1994.

———, ed. *Off the Record: The Private Papers of Harry S. Truman.* New York: Harper & Row, 1980.

———, ed. *Truman in the White House: The Diary of Eben A. Ayers.* Columbia: University of Missouri Press, 1991.

Foreign Relations of the United States, 1947. Vol. 5, *The Near East and Africa.* Washington, D.C.: United States Government Printing Office, 1971.

Forrestal, James. *The Forrestal Diaries.* Edited by Walter Millis with E. S. Duffield. New York: Viking Press, 1951.

Gaddis, John Lewis. *The United States and the Origins of the Cold War, 1941–1947.* New York: Columbia University Press, 1972.

———. "Was the Truman Doctrine a Real Turning Point?" *Foreign Affairs* 52 (1974): 386–402.

———. *We Now Know: Rethinking Cold War History.* Oxford: Clarendon Press, 1997.

George, Alexander L. *Managing U.S.-Soviet Rivalry.* Boulder, Colo.: Westview, 1983.

Gerolymatos, Andre. *Red Acropolis, Black Terror: The Greek Civil War and the Origins of Soviet-American Rivalry, 1943–1949.* New York: Basic Books, 2004.

Goldman, Eric F. *The Crucial Decade.* New York: Alfred Knopf, 1959.

Gregg, Richard B. "Embodied Meaning in American Public Discourse during the Cold War." *Metaphorical World Politics.* Edited by Francis A. Beer and Christ'l De Landtsheer, 59–73. East Lansing: Michigan State University Press, 2004.

———. "Kenneth Burke's Prolegomena to the Study of the Rhetoric of Form." *Communication Quarterly* 26 (1978): 3–13.

Halle, Louis. *The Cold War as History.* New York: Harper & Row, 1967.

Hamby, Alonzo L. "Harry S. Truman and the Origins of the Truman Doctrine." In *The Truman Doctrine of Aid to Greece: A Fifty-Year Retrospective.* Edited by Eugene T. Rossides, 12–23. New York and Washington, D.C.: Academy of Political Science and American Hellenic Institute Foundation, 1998.

———. *Man of the People: A Life of Harry S. Truman.* New York: Oxford University Press, 1995.

Harbutt, Fraser J. *The Iron Curtain: Churchill, America, and the Origins of the Cold War.* New York: Oxford University Press, 1986.

Hart, Roderick P. *Verbal Style and the Presidency: A Computer-Based Analysis.* Orlando, Fla.: Academic, 1984.

Hartmann, Susan M. *Truman and the 80th Congress.* Columbia: University of Missouri Press, 1971.

Hinds, Lynn Boyd, and Theodore Otto Windt Jr. *The Cold War as Rhetoric: The Beginnings, 1945–1950.* Westport, Conn.: Praeger, 1991.

Hogan, Michael J. *A Cross of Iron: Harry S. Truman and the Origins of the National Security State, 1945–1954.* Cambridge, U.K.: Cambridge University Press, 1998.

Huget, Jennifer. "The Secret Heart of Harry Truman; Diary Reveals Diagnosis of 'Cardiac Asthma': Hushed-Up Then, Obscure Still." *Washington Post,* July 22, 2003, Sec. F, 1.

Ivie, Robert L. *Democracy and America's War on Terror.* Tuscaloosa: University of Alabama Press, 2005.

———. "Fire, Flood, and Red Fever: Motivating Metaphors of Global Emergency in the Truman Doctrine Speech." *Presidential Studies Quarterly* 29 (1999): 570–91.

———. "The Ideology of Freedom's 'Fragility' in American Foreign Policy Argument." *Journal of the American Forensic Association* 24 (1987): 27–36.

———. "Literalizing the Metaphor of Soviet Savagery: President Truman's Plain Style." *Southern Speech Communication Journal* 51 (1986): 91–105.

———. "Realism Masking Fear: George F. Kennan's Political Rhetoric." *Post-Realism: The Rhetorical Turn in International Relations.* Edited by Francis A. Beer and Robert Hariman, 55–74. East Lansing: Michigan State University Press, 1996.

Jones, Howard. "A Reassessment of the Truman Doctrine and Its Impact on Greece and U.S. Foreign Policy." In *The Truman Doctrine of Aid to Greece: A Fifty-Year Retrospective.* Edited by Eugene Rossides, 24–41. New York and Washington, D.C.: Academy of Political Science and American Hellenic Institute Foundation, 1998.

Jones, Joseph Marion. *The Fifteen Weeks: An Inside Account of the Genesis of the Marshall Plan.* New York: Harbinger, 1955.

Kennan, George F. *Memoirs: 1925–1950.* Boston: Little, Brown, 1967.

Krock, Arthur. *Memoirs: Sixty Years on the Firing Line.* New York: Funk & Wagnalls, 1968.

———. "Mr. Kennedy's Management of the News." *Fortune,* March 1963, 82, 199.

Kuniholm, Bruce Robellet. *The Origins of the Cold War in the Near East.* Princeton: Princeton University Press, 1980.

Lakoff, George, and Mark Johnson. *Metaphors We Live By.* Chicago: University of Chicago Press, 1980.

Lanham, Richard A. *A Handlist of Rhetorical Terms.* 2d ed. Berkeley: University of California Press, 1991.

Larson, Deborah Welch. *Origins of Containment.* Princeton: Princeton University Press, 1985.

Leffler, Melvyn P. *A Preponderance of Power: National Security, the Truman Administration, and the Cold War.* Stanford, Calif.: Stanford University Press, 1992.

Liddell and Scott's Greek-English Lexicon. Abridged ed.; Oxford: Oxford University Press, 1977.

Massing, Michael. "Now They Tell Us." Editorial. *New York Review of Books.* February 26, 2004: 1, 3. http://www.nybooks.com/articles/16922.

May, Ernest R. *"Lessons" of the Past: The Use and Misuse of History in American Foreign Policy.* New York: Oxford University Press, 1973.

McCullough, David. *Truman.* New York: Simon and Schuster, 1992.

McFarland, Stephen L. "The Iranian Crisis of 1946 and the Onset of the Cold War." In *Origins of the Cold War: An International History.* Edited by Melvyn P. Leffler and David S. Painter, 239–56. London and New York: Routledge, 1994.

McKerrow, Ray E. "Truman and Korea: Rhetoric in the Pursuit of Victory." *Central States Speech Journal* 28 (1977): 1–12.

McMahon, Robert J. "'By Helping Others, We Help Ourselves': The Cold War Rhetoric of American Foreign Policy." In *Critical Reflections on the Cold War: Linking Rhetoric and History.* Edited by Martin J. Medhurst and H. W. Brands, 233–46. College Station: Texas A&M University Press, 2000.

Medhurst, Martin J. "Introduction: The Rhetorical Construction of History." In *Critical Reflections on the Cold War: Linking Rhetoric and History.* Edited by Martin J. Medhurst and H. W. Brands, 3–19. College Station: Texas A&M University Press, 2000.

———. "Rhetoric and Cold War: A Strategic Approach." In *Cold War Rhetoric: Strategy, Metaphor, and Ideology.* Edited by Martin J. Medhurst, Robert L. Ivie, Philip Wander, and Robert L. Scott, 19–27. New York: Greenwood, 1990.

———. "Truman's Rhetorical Reticence, 1945–1947: An Interpretive Essay." *Quarterly Journal of Speech* 75 (1988): 52–70.

Medline Plus Medical Dictionary. http://www2.merriam-webster. com/cgi-bin/mwmednlm.

Miles, Donna. "Rumsfeld Cites Truman as Inspiration for Nation Today." March 2, 2006. American Forces Information Service News Articles. LexisNexis.

Miscamble, Wilson D., C.S.C. *George F. Kennan and the Making of American Foreign Policy, 1947–1950.* Princeton: Princeton University Press, 1992.

Newman, Robert P. "NSC (National Insecurity) 68: Nitze's Second Hallucination." In *Critical Reflections on the Cold War: Linking Rhetoric and History.* Edited by Martin J. Medhurst and H. W. Brands, 55–94. College Station: Texas A&M University Press.

Offner, Arnold A. *Another Such Victory: President Truman and the Cold War, 1945–1953.* Stanford, Calif.: Stanford University Press, 2002.

Ojserkis, Raymond P. *Beginnings of the Cold War Arms Race: The Truman Administration and the U.S. Arms Build-Up.* Westport, Conn.: Praeger, 2003.

Painter, David S. *The Cold War: An International History.* London and New York: Routledge, 1999.

Parry-Giles, Shawn J. *The Rhetorical Presidency, Propaganda, and the Cold War, 1945–1955.* Westport, Conn.: Praeger, 2002.

Paterson, Thomas G. *Meeting the Communist Threat.* New York: Oxford University Press, 1988.

Pierce, Anne Rice. *Woodrow Wilson and Harry Truman: Mission and Power in American Foreign Policy.* Westport, Conn.: Praeger, 2003.

Pogue, Forrest. *George C. Marshall: Statesman, 1945–1959.* New York: Viking Penguin, 1987.

Public Papers of the Presidents, Presidential Years of 1945–1969. Washington, D.C.: United States Government Printing Office, 1958–70.

Reuters News Service. "Greek Protesters Topple Truman Statue in Anti-War Demo." Boston.com News. www.boston.com/news/world/europe/articles/2006/07/25/greek_protesters_topple_truman_statue_in_anti_war_demo.

Robertson, David. *Sly and Able: A Political Biography of James F. Byrnes.* New York: W. W. Norton, 1994.

Ryan, Halford R. *Harry S. Truman: Presidential Rhetoric.* Westport, Conn.: Greenwood, 1993.

Schapsmeier, Edward L., and Frederick H. Schapsmeier. *Prophet in Politics: Henry A. Wallace and the War Years, 1940–1965.* Ames: Iowa State University Press, 1970.

Scott, Robert L. "Cold War Rhetoric: Conceptually and Critically." In *Cold War Rhetoric: Strategy, Metaphor, and Ideology.* Edited by Martin J. Medhurst, Robert L. Ivie, Philip Wander, and Robert L. Scott, 1–16. New York: Greenwood, 1990.

Shafer, Kenneth, MD. Interviews with Author. June 23, 2006. July 14, 2006.

Shimko, Keith L. "The Power of Metaphors and the Metaphors of Power: The United States in the Cold War and After." In *Metaphorical World Politics.* Edited by Francis A. Beer and Christ'l De Landtsheer, 199–215. East Lansing: Michigan State University Press, 2004.

Stalin, Joseph. "Analysis of Victory." February 9, 1946. In *A Documentary History of Communism.* Vol. 2. Edited by Robert V. Daniels, 142–47. New York: Random House, 1960.

Stoler, Mark A. *George C. Marshall: Soldier-Statesman of the American Century.* Boston: Twayne, 1989.

Stuart, Graham H. *The Department of State: A History of Its Organization, Procedure, and Personnel.* New York: Macmillan, 1949.

Thompson, K. W. *Ten Presidents and the Press.* Lanham, Md.: University Press of America, 1983.

Truman, Harry S. *Memoirs.* Vol. 1, *Year of Decisions.* Garden City, N.Y.: Doubleday, 1955.

———. *Memoirs.* Vol. 2, *Years of Trial and Hope.* Garden City, N.Y.: Doubleday, 1956.

———. "Special Message to the Congress on Greece and Turkey: The Truman Doctrine." March 12, 1947. Audio recording. Available: from www.americanrhetoric.com.

Truman, Margaret. *Bess W. Truman.* New York: Macmillan, 1986.

———. *Harry S. Truman.* New York: William Morrow, 1973.

Truman, Margaret, with Margaret Cousins. *Souvenir: Margaret Truman's Own Story.* New York: McGraw-Hill, 1956.

Tudda, Chris. "'Reenacting the Story of Tantalus': Eisenhower, Dulles, and the Failed Rhetoric of Liberation." *Journal of Cold War Studies* 7 (2005): 3–35.

Ulam, Adam B. *The Rivals: America & Russia since World War II.* New York: Viking, 1971. Reprint, New York: Penguin, 1976.

Underhill, Robert. *The Truman Persuasions.* Ames: Iowa State University Press, 1981.

Vandenberg, Arthur. *The Private Papers of Senator Vandenberg.* Edited by Arthur H. Vandenberg Jr., with Joe Alex Morris. Boston: Houghton Mifflin, 1952.

Wallace, Henry. "The Way to Peace." In *Henry Wallace, Harry Truman, and the Cold War.* Edited by Richard J. Walton, 100–108. New York: Viking, 1976.

Walton, Richard J. *Henry Wallace, Harry Truman, and the Cold War.* New York: Viking, 1976.

Weekly Compilation of Presidential Documents. Washington, D.C.: Office of the Federal Register, National Archives and Records Services, General Services Administration. 1990, 2001.

West, J. B., with Mary Lynn Kotz. *Upstairs at the White House: My Life with the First Ladies.* New York: Coward, McCann, and Geoghegan, 1973.

White, Eugene E., and Clair R. Henderlider. "What Harry Truman Told Us about His Speaking." *Quarterly Journal of Speech* 40 (February 1954): 37–42.

White, Graham, and John Maze. *Henry A. Wallace: His Search for a New World Order.* Chapel Hill: University of North Carolina Press, 1995.

Wilson, Woodrow. "Address to Congress." April 2, 1917. In *War Addresses of Woodrow Wilson.* Edited by Arthur Roy Leonard, 32–45. Boston: Ginn, 1918.

Winkler, Carol K. *In the Name of Terrorism: Presidents on Political Violence in the Post–World War II Era.* Albany: State University of New York Press, 2006.

Woods, Randall B., and Howard Jones. *Dawning of the Cold War: The United States' Quest for Order.* Athens: University of Georgia Press, 1991.

Zarefsky, David. "The Rhetorical Cold War: A Response to Professor Norman A. Graebner." Fourth Annual Conference on Presidential Rhetoric. Texas A&M University. March 5, 1998.

INDEX

ISBN-13: 978-1-60344-032-5
ISBN-10: 1-60344-032-1